The Quick-Bread Cook Book

Loaves of Fun!

by

Nancy K. Adams

GOLDEN WEST ☼ PUBLISHERS

Front cover photo by Tom Vano/PhotoBank, Inc.

Back cover and interior illustrations by Mark Woodruff

ISBN 1-885590-21-0

Printed in the United States of America

Golden West Publishers, Inc.
4113 N. Longview Ave.
Phoenix, AZ 85014, USA

(602) 265-4392

Table of Contents

Loaves of Fun!

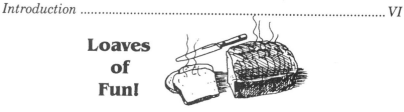

Butters & Spreads

Muffins

Meet the Author

Nancy Kerr Adams is enticed by the wonderful smell of bread baking. Constantly experimenting to create new, tasty and healthy breads, she has had fun loafing all the way through this book.

She has a master's degree in communications from the University of Tulsa, which she used in the field of advertising in New York and in Colorado Springs before becoming a financial consultant with Merrill Lynch in California.

Nancy has three children; is an artist and a free lance writer in various media. She lives with her husband, Richard, in Indian Wells, California and Pagosa Springs, Colorado.

Introduction

The many varieties of tasteful, colorful and unusual recipes in this book will add that very special touch to your meals. Your family and friends will be amazed that you have been able to prepare that time honored favorite *Homemade Bread!*

With these recipes, you will find that you can prepare any of the many choices easily and *in only minutes!* Please be sure to read the General Information pages starting at page 98 — especially the section on *Speedy Preparation Tips!* to get your breadmaking off on the right track. *Flavored Butters and Spreads* on pages 67 and 68 will add that special touch to ensure rave reviews for your culinary prowess!

Loaves

Almond-Banana Loaves

Beat together:
**2 cups puréed BANANAS
1/2 cup SALAD OIL
1/4 cup SUGAR
1/3 cup firmly packed BROWN SUGAR
2 EGGS, beaten
1/2 tsp. VANILLA**

Combine:
**2 cups FLOUR
1 tsp. BAKING SODA
1/2 tsp. BAKING POWDER
1/2 tsp. SALT**

Stir flour mixture into banana mixture until just moist.

Add:
1 cup finely chopped ALMONDS

Split between 3 sprayed 6 x 3 loaf pans. Bake at 350° for 50 minutes.

Apple-Walnut Loaves

Cream:
>**3 Tbsp. BUTTER or MARGARINE, room temperature**
>**1/3 cup SUGAR**

Blend into creamed mixture:
>**1/2 cup BROWN SUGAR**
>**1 EGG, well beaten**
>**1 tsp. VANILLA**
>**3 cups peeled and finely diced APPLES**
>**1/2 cup BUTTERMILK or YOGURT**

Sift together:
>**1 3/4 cups FLOUR**
>**1/2 tsp. CINNAMON**
>**1/2 tsp. NUTMEG**
>**1/2 tsp. SALT**
>**1 tsp. BAKING SODA**

Combine mixtures until just moist.

Stir in:
>**1/2 cup chopped WALNUTS**

Spoon into sprayed 9 x 5 loaf pan. Bake at 350° for one hour. This is a moist bread. It has true nut bread consistency and a spicy flavor with lots of apple.

Serve hot
or at room
temperature the
next day!

Green Apple-Walnut Loaves

Mix together:
1 3/4 cups FLOUR
1/4 cup cracked WHEAT
1 tsp. BAKING SODA
1 tsp. BAKING POWDER
1 tsp. SALT
1 tsp. CINNAMON
1/4 tsp. GINGER

Whisk together:
2 EGGS
1/2 cup SALAD OIL
1 tsp. VANILLA

Toss together:
3 cups peeled and finely diced tart GREEN APPLES
3/4 cup SUGAR

Stir egg mixture into apples, add flour mixture, mix until just moistened.

Add:
1 cup RAISINS
1 cup chopped WALNUTS

Divide into four 6 x 3 sprayed loaf pans. Bake at 350° for 50 minutes.

Applesauce Loaves

Mix together:
- 2 1/4 cups FLOUR
- 3/4 tsp. BAKING SODA
- 3/4 tsp. NUTMEG
- 1 tsp. CINNAMON
- 1/2 tsp. SALT
- 1/2 tsp. BAKING POWDER

Combine:
- 1 1/4 cups APPLESAUCE
- 1/3 cup SUGAR
- 1/4 cup BROWN SUGAR
- 1 EGG
- 1/3 cup melted BUTTER

Combine mixtures until just blended.

Fold in:
- 1 cup chopped PECANS
- 3/4 cup RAISINS

Pour into sprayed 9 x 5 loaf pan. Bake at 350° for one hour 10 minutes. This makes a nice, large loaf. It is moist and has a good, delicate flavor. It has good consistency and holds its moisture well.

Applesauce-Banana Loaves

Cream:
- 4 Tbsp. BUTTER or MARGARINE, room temperature
- 1/2 cup SUGAR

Add:
- 2 EGGS, beaten
- 3 Tbsp. SOUR MILK
- 1 mashed BANANA
- 1 1/4 cups APPLESAUCE

Sift together:
- 2 cups FLOUR
- 1 tsp. BAKING SODA
- 3/4 tsp. SALT

Blend mixtures until just moist. Pour into sprayed 9 x 5 loaf pan. Bake at 350° for one hour 15 minutes. This is a very moist bread with a good combination of fruit flavors. It keeps well.

Applesauce-Oatmeal Loaves

Sift together:
1 1/3 cups FLOUR
1/2 cup SUGAR
1 tsp. SALT
1 tsp. BAKING POWDER
1 tsp. BAKING SODA
1/2 tsp. CINNAMON
1/4 tsp. NUTMEG

Combine:
1 cup OATS (fast cooking)
1/2 cup RAISINS
1 1/2 cups APPLESAUCE
1/3 cup SALAD OIL
2 EGGS
1/4 cup MILK
1/4 cup BROWN SUGAR

Combine mixtures until just moistened.

Stir in:
1/2 cup chopped PECANS

Pour into sprayed 9 x 5 loaf pan.

Combine and sprinkle over batter:
2 Tbsp. BROWN SUGAR
2 Tbsp. finely chopped PECANS
1/4 tsp. CINNAMON

Bake at 350° for one hour.

Apricot Loaves

Sift together:
> **2 cups FLOUR**
> **1 1/2 tsp. BAKING POWDER**
> **1/2 tsp. BAKING SODA**
> **1/2 tsp. SALT**

Cream:
> **1/2 cup BUTTER, room temperature**
> **1/2 cup SUGAR**

Beat in:
> **2 EGGS**
> **1 cup drained and puréed APRICOT HALVES**
> **3 Tbsp. ORANGE JUICE**

Combine mixtures.

Stir in:
> **1/2 cup chopped WALNUTS**

Pour into sprayed 9 x 5 loaf pan. Bake at 350° for 40 to 50 minutes. This bread has a butter cake flavor. Served warm, it is cakelike and light in texture.

Apricot-Date Loaves

Combine:
> **2 cups sifted FLOUR**
> **1 tsp. BAKING POWDER**
> **1/2 tsp. BAKING SODA**
> **1/2 tsp. SALT**
> **1/2 tsp. NUTMEG**

Combine:
> **1/2 cup BUTTER, melted**
> **1/3 cup SUGAR**
> **2 EGGS, beaten**
> **4 Tbsp. ORANGE JUICE**

Combine mixtures until just blended.

Stir in:
> **1/2 cup finely chopped DRIED APRICOTS**
> **1/2 cup finely chopped DATES**
> **1/2 cup chopped WALNUTS**

Pour into sprayed 9 x 5 loaf pan. Bake one hour at 350°.

Apricot-Raisin-Sunflower Loaves

Mix together:
1 1/2 cups FLOUR	**1 tsp. CINNAMON**
1/2 cup WHEAT FLOUR	**1/4 tsp. NUTMEG**
2 tsp. BAKING POWDER	**1/2 tsp. SALT**

Combine:
1 cup MILK	**1 EGG, beaten**
3/4 cup HONEY	**1/4 cup SALAD OIL**

Combine mixtures until just moist.

Fold in:
> **3/4 cup finely chopped DRIED APRICOTS**
> **1/2 cup RAISINS**
> **1/2 cup chopped SUNFLOWER SEEDS**

Pour into sprayed 9 x 5 loaf pan. Bake one hour at 350°.

Apricot Preserve Loaves

Combine:
> **2 1/4 cups FLOUR**
> **1/2 cup BROWN SUGAR**
> **1 Tbsp. BAKING POWDER**

Cut in:
> **1/2 cup MARGARINE or BUTTER, room temperature**

Combine:
> **1/2 cup MILK**
> **1 EGG, beaten**
> **1 cup APRICOT PRESERVES**

Combine mixtures until just moist.

Add:
> **1 cup chopped PECANS**

Pour into two 8 x 4 sprayed loaf pans. Bake at 350° for one hour. This bread is moist and not too sweet. Serve warm.

Apricot-Orange Loaves

Mix together in order:
- 2 1/4 cups FLOUR
- 3/4 cup SUGAR
- 1 Tbsp. BAKING POWDER
- 1/2 tsp. BAKING SODA
- 1 tsp. SALT
- 3 Tbsp. SALAD OIL
- 2 EGGS
- 1/2 cup MILK
- 3/4 cup ORANGE JUICE
- 4 tsp. grated ORANGE PEEL
- 1 cup chopped NUTS
- 1 cup finely chopped DRIED APRICOTS

Pour into sprayed 9 x 5 loaf pan. Bake at 350° for one hour. This colorful bread looks great sliced.

Avocado-Pineapple Loaves

Blend:
- 1 3/4 cups FLOUR, sifted
- 1/2 cup SUGAR
- 1 tsp. BAKING SODA
- 1/2 tsp. BAKING POWDER
- 1/2 tsp. SALT

Combine:
- 1/2 cup SALAD OIL
- 1/2 cup mashed AVOCADO
- 1/2 cup crushed PINEAPPLE
- 2 EGGS, beaten
- 1 tsp. VANILLA

Add:
- 1/2 cup chopped PECANS

Blend mixtures until just moistened and then pour into sprayed 9 x 5 loaf pan. Bake at 350° for 50 to 60 minutes.

Avocado Loaves

Cream:
>**1/2 cup BUTTER or MARGARINE, room temperature**

Add and beat until fluffy:
>**1 cup SUGAR**

Add one at a time:
>**3 EGGS**

Sift together:
>**2 cups FLOUR**
>**2 tsp. CINNAMON**
>**3/4 tsp. SALT**
>**3/4 tsp. ALLSPICE**
>**1 1/2 tsp. BAKING SODA**

Combine:
>**3/4 to 1 cup puréed AVOCADOS**
>**1 1/2 tsp. VANILLA**
>**3/4 cup BUTTERMILK or, 4 1/2 Tbsp. POWDERED**
>   **BUTTERMILK and 3/4 cup WATER or, YOGURT**

Blend all mixtures until just moist.

Stir in:
>**1/2 cup chopped PECANS**
>**3/4 cup RAISINS**

Pour into two sprayed 8 x 4 loaf pans. Bake at 350° for one hour.

Good texture, moist & cakelike. Delicious!

Bacon-Cheddar Loaves

Combine:
> 2 cups FLOUR
> 1/3 cup YELLOW CORNMEAL
> 1 tsp. SALT
> 1/2 tsp. BAKING SODA
> 2 tsp. BAKING POWDER

Combine:
> 1/4 cup BUTTER or MARGARINE, room temperature
> 2 Tbsp. SUGAR
> 2 EGGS, beaten
> 1 cup BUTTERMILK or YOGURT
> 1/2 cup grated CHEDDAR CHEESE
> 1 tsp. WORCESTERSHIRE SAUCE
> 1 cup chopped, crisp BACON
> 2 Tbsp. minced ONIONS

Combine mixtures until moist. Split between 3 sprayed 6 x 3 loaf pans. Bake at 350° for 45 minutes.

Banana-Nut Loaves

Cream:
> 1/2 cup BUTTER or MARGARINE, room temperature

Add and beat until well blended:
> 3/4 cup BROWN SUGAR
> 1/4 cup SUGAR
> 1 EGG
> 1/2 tsp. VANILLA
> 3/4 cup mashed BANANA

Combine, then add to banana mixture:
> 1 cup FLOUR
> 1 tsp. BAKING POWDER
> 1/2 tsp. CINNAMON

Mix until just moistened. Pour into 8 x 4 sprayed loaf pan.

Sprinkle with:
> 1/2 cup chopped NUTS

Bake at 350° for 55 minutes.

Banana-Almond Loaves

Beat together:
>**1 cup mashed BANANAS**
>**1/4 cup SUGAR**
>**1 EGG**
>**1/4 cup MILK**
>**2 cups BISCUIT MIX**

Measure:
>**1/2 cup plus 2 Tbsp. melted BUTTER**
>**1/2 cup BROWN SUGAR**
>**1/2 cup sliced and lightly toasted ALMONDS**
>**1 3/4 tsp. CINNAMON**
>**1/4 tsp. NUTMEG**

Pour half of the melted butter into 9 x 5 loaf pan. Sprinkle with 1/4 cup brown sugar and 1/4 cup almonds. Mix together the remaining brown sugar and almonds with the cinnamon and nutmeg. Spoon half of banana mixture in pan. Add layer of brown sugar mixture. Drizzle with remaining melted butter. Spoon remaining batter on top. Bake at 375° for 50 minutes. This bread looks good served down side up.

Banana-Apricot Loaves

Combine:
>**3/4 cup mashed BANANAS**
>**1/2 cup MILK**
>**1 EGG, beaten**
>**1/4 cup melted BUTTER**
>**1/3 cup SUGAR**
>**1/2 cup BROWN SUGAR**
>**1/2 cup chopped, DRIED APRICOTS**
>**1/2 cup chopped NUTS**

Sift together:
>**2 cups FLOUR**
>**1 tsp. BAKING POWDER**
>**1/2 tsp. SALT**
>**1/2 tsp. BAKING SODA**

Combine mixtures, stirring until just blended. Pour into sprayed 9 x 5 loaf pan. Bake at 350° for one hour.

Banana-Bran Loaves

Combine:
> 1 EGG, well beaten
> 1 1/2 cups mashed BANANAS
> 1/4 cup melted BUTTER or MARGARINE
> 1 cup BRAN KERNELS
> 1/2 cup BROWN SUGAR

Sift together:
> 1 1/2 cups FLOUR, sifted
> 2 1/2 tsp. BAKING POWDER
> 1/2 tsp. BAKING SODA
> 1/2 tsp. SALT

Combine both mixtures, stirring just enough to dampen all flour.
Add:
> 1/2 cup chopped PECANS or WALNUTS

Turn into sprayed 9 x 5 loaf pan. Bake at 350° for one hour.

Banana-Oat Bran Loaves

Cream:
> 1/2 cup BUTTER or MARGARINE, room temperature

Add and beat until fluffy:
> 3/4 cup BROWN SUGAR
> 2/3 cup SUGAR
> 1 1/4 tsp. ALLSPICE
> 1/2 tsp. NUTMEG

Mix in:
> 2 EGGS
> 1 1/2 tsp. VANILLA

Combine:
> 1 1/2 cups FLOUR
> 3/4 cup OAT BRAN
> 3/4 tsp. BAKING SODA
> 3/4 tsp. BAKING POWDER
> 1/4 tsp. SALT

Add dry ingredients alternately to butter mixture with:
> 1/2 cup SOUR CREAM
> 1 1/4 cups mashed BANANAS

Pour into sprayed 9 x 5 loaf pan.
Sprinkle with:
> 1/2 cup chopped NUTS

Bake at 350° for one hour.

Banana Quick-to-Mix Loaves

Mix well:

- **1 1/2 cups mashed BANANAS (about 3)**
- **3 cups BISCUIT MIX**
- **3/4 cup SUGAR**
- **1/2 cup MILK**
- **1 EGG**
- **3/4 cup chopped NUTS**

Pour into 9 x 5 sprayed loaf pan.
Bake at 350° for one hour.

I love banana bread!

Banana-Sour Milk Loaves

Cream:

- **2/3 cup BUTTER or MARGARINE, room temperature**
- **1 1/4 cups SUGAR**

Add:

- **1 1/4 cups mashed BANANAS**
- **2/3 cup SOUR MILK***

Mix together and add to banana mixture:

- **2 1/2 cups FLOUR**
- **1 1/4 tsp. BAKING POWDER**
- **1 1/4 tsp. BAKING SODA**
- **1 tsp. SALT**

Stir in:

- **2/3 cup chopped NUTS**

Put into 2 sprayed 8 x 4 loaf pans. Bake at 350° for 45 to 50 minutes.

*To sour milk, add 2 teaspoons vinegar to the 2 / 3 cup of milk (at room temperature). Let sit 5 minutes. This creates a good bread texture that is moist and has good flavor.

Banana-Wheat Loaves

Blend until smooth:
> 1/2 cup BUTTER or MARGARINE, melted
> 2 EGGS, beaten
> 1 1/2 cups mashed BANANAS (2 to 4)
> 1/2 cup SUGAR
> 1/2 cup BROWN SUGAR

Sift together and add to banana mixture:
> 1 cup FLOUR
> 1 cup WHEAT FLOUR
> 1/2 tsp. SALT
> 1 tsp. BAKING SODA

Stir in:
> 3/4 cup chopped WALNUTS

Turn into 2 sprayed 8 x 4 loaf pans. Bake at 325° for one hour 10 minutes. Very good flavor with wheat texture.

Beer Loaves

Combine:
> 3 cups SELF-RISING FLOUR, unsifted
> 2 Tbsp. SUGAR
> 1/3 cup grated CHEDDAR CHEESE
> 1 Tbsp. grated ONION

Add and blend:
> 12 oz. BEER, room temperature

Spread into sprayed 9 x 5 loaf pan.

Brush with:
> 1 EGG, beaten with 1 Tbsp. WATER

Bake on lowest shelf in oven at 350° for one hour. Brush top with melted butter. Excellent cocktail or dinner bread. Good crust with light texture beneath. The yeasty flavor smacks of sour dough bread.

Blueberry-Nut Loaves

Mix together:
>   **2 cups FLOUR**
>   **2 tsp. BAKING POWDER**
>   **1/2 tsp. SALT**
>   **1 tsp. CINNAMON**

Cream:
>   **1/2 cup BUTTER, room temperature**
>   **3/4 cup SUGAR**

Beat in:
>   **2 EGGS**
>   **1/2 cup MILK**

Combine mixtures until just moist.

Stir in:
>   **2 cups rinsed and drained BLUEBERRIES**
>   **2 Tbsp. LEMON JUICE, pour over berries**
>   **1/2 cup chopped WALNUTS or PECANS**

Pour into sprayed 9 x 5 loaf pan. Bake at 350° for one hour.

Blueberry-Orange Loaves

Beat until creamy:
>   **1/2 cup BUTTER**
>   **3/4 cup SUGAR**

Add one at a time:
>   **2 EGGS**

Combine:
>   **2 cups FLOUR**   **1/2 tsp. BAKING SODA**
>   **2 tsp. BAKING POWDER**   **1/2 tsp. SALT**
>   **1 tsp. CINNAMON**   **1/2 tsp. GROUND**
>   **1 tsp. ORANGE PEEL**   **CLOVES**

Add flour mixture alternately to batter with:
>   **2/3 cup ORANGE JUICE**

Stir in:
>   **2 cups drained and rinsed BLUEBERRIES**
>   **3/4 cup chopped PECANS**

Pour into 2 sprayed 8 x 4 loaf pans. Bake at 350° for 50 minutes.

Brazil Nut Loaves

Sift together:
>1 cup FLOUR
>1 cup WHEAT FLOUR
>1/3 cup SUGAR
>3/4 tsp. BAKING SODA
>1/2 tsp. SALT

Add and blend:
>1/4 cup MOLASSES, unsulphured
>3/4 cup BUTTERMILK or YOGURT
>1 EGG, beaten

Fold in:
>1/2 cup RAISINS
>1/2 cup chopped BRAZIL NUTS

Pour into sprayed 9 x 5 loaf pan. Bake at 350° for one hour.

Light Brown Bread Loaves

Stir together:
>1 cup FLOUR
>1 cup WHEAT FLOUR
>1 3/4 tsp. BAKING POWDER
>1/4 tsp. BAKING SODA
>3/4 tsp. SALT
>1/2 cup BROWN SUGAR
>1/2 cup finely chopped WALNUTS

Beat together:
>1 EGG, lightly beaten
>1 1/3 cups MILK

Combine mixtures until just moistened. Turn into 9 x 5 sprayed loaf pan or 2 sprayed 8 x 4 loaf pans. Bake at 350° for 50 minutes. This bread has good texture. It is not too sweet, more like bread than cake.

Raisin-Brown Bread Loaves

Mix together:
- **1 cup FLOUR**
- **1 1/2 cup WHEAT GERM**
- **3 Tbsp. SUGAR**
- **3/4 tsp. SALT**
- **1/2 tsp. BAKING POWDER**
- **1/2 tsp. BAKING SODA**
- **1 cup MILK**
- **1 EGG**
- **1/4 cup MOLASSES**
- **1/2 cup chopped NUTS**
- **1/2 cup chopped RAISINS**
- **1/4 cup SALAD OIL**

Pour into sprayed 9 x 5 loaf pan. Bake at 350° for one hour.

Buttermilk Bread Loaves

Sift together:
- **2 cups FLOUR**
- **2 tsp. BAKING POWDER**
- **1/2 tsp. BAKING SODA**
- **1/2 tsp. SALT**
- **1/2 tsp. CINNAMON**
- **1/4 tsp. NUTMEG**

Combine:
- **1 EGG, slightly beaten**
- **1 cup BUTTERMILK**
- **1 Tbsp. BUTTER, melted**

Stir in:
- **1 cup BROWN SUGAR**
- **1 cup chopped PECANS**

Combine mixtures until just moistened. Bake in sprayed 9 x 5 loaf pan. Bake at 350° for 45 minutes or more.

Buttermilk-Sesame Loaves

Sift together:
2 cups FLOUR
1 1/2 tsp. BAKING POWDER
1/2 tsp. BAKING SODA
1/2 tsp. SALT

Combine and add to flour mixture:
2 Tbsp. SESAME SEEDS
2 Tbsp. SUGAR
1/4 tsp. CINNAMON
1/4 tsp. NUTMEG

Mix together:
2 EGGS, beaten
1 cup SUGAR
3 Tbsp. melted BUTTER

Add flour mixture to egg mixture alternately with:
1 cup BUTTERMILK (until just blended)

Stir in:
3/4 cup chopped WALNUTS

Pour into 2 sprayed 8 x 4 loaf pans. Bake at 350° for 50 to 55 minutes. This has a nice, light texture and good flavor served warm.

Candied Fruit Loaves

Sift together:
2 cups FLOUR
1 tsp. BAKING POWDER
1 tsp. BAKING SODA
1/2 tsp. SALT
1/2 cup SUGAR

Blend:
2 EGGS, lightly beaten
1/2 cup MILK
3/4 tsp. ANISE or ALMOND EXTRACT

Combine mixtures until just moist.

Fold in:
3/4 cup chopped WALNUTS
1/2 cup chopped CANDIED FRUIT

Pour into 2 sprayed 8 x 4 loaf pans. Bake at 350° for one hour.

Caraway Loaves

Mix together:
- 3/4 cup WHOLE WHEAT FLOUR
- 1 cup FLOUR
- 1/2 tsp. BAKING SODA
- 1 tsp. SALT
- 1 Tbsp. CARAWAY SEEDS
- 1 Tbsp. BROWN SUGAR

Add:
- 1/3 cup BUTTER, melted
- 1/3 cup OATS
- 1 cup BUTTERMILK

Combine lightly until mixture is smooth. Knead until soft but not sticky. Turn out on a floured board. Divide into three or four portions. Flatten and shape round. Place on a cookie sheet and score with a knife dipped in cold water or flour. Bake at 400° for 20 minutes. Serve warm with butter and jams or preserves.

Caraway Raisin Loaves

Sift together:
- 2 cups FLOUR
- 2 tsp. BAKING POWDER
- 1/2 tsp. SALT

Add:
- 1/2 cup SUGAR

Cut in to texture of coarse cornmeal:
- 1/4 cup BUTTER or MARGARINE

Combine:
- 2 EGGS, beaten
- 1 cup MILK

Combine mixtures until just moistened, then stir in:
- 1/2 cup RAISINS
- 1 Tbsp. CARAWAY SEEDS

Pour into 9 x 5 sprayed loaf pan. Bake at 350° for one hour.

Carrot Loaves

Combine:
2 cups FLOUR, sifted
1 tsp. BAKING POWDER
3/4 tsp. BAKING SODA
1/2 tsp. SALT
1 tsp. CINNAMON

Combine, beat until smooth:
1/2 cup SUGAR
1/2 cup BROWN SUGAR
3/4 cup SALAD OIL

Add one at a time:
2 EGGS
1 1/2 cups grated CARROTS

Combine mixtures until just blended.

Fold in:
1/2 cup chopped PECANS

Pour into a 9 x 5 sprayed loaf pan, and an 8 x 4 sprayed loaf pan. Bake at 350° for one hour. A cream cheese spread goes well with this bread.

Easy Carrot Loaves

This is an all-time favorite!

Mix together:
2 cups FLOUR, sifted
2 tsp. BAKING SODA
1 tsp. SALT
2 tsp. CINNAMON
1 cup SUGAR
1/2 cup BROWN SUGAR

Mix together:
1/2 cup SALAD OIL
4 EGGS, well beaten
1/2 cup chopped PECANS
2 (7 1/2 oz.) jars junior size CARROTS (baby food)

Combine mixtures until just blended. Pour into 2 sprayed 8 x 4 loaf pans. Bake at 375° for one hour.

Carrot-Spice Loaves

Mix together:
2 cups FLOUR
1 tsp. BAKING POWDER
1 tsp. BAKING SODA
1 tsp. SALT
1/4 tsp. ALLSPICE
1 tsp. CINNAMON
1/8 tsp. ground CLOVES
1/8 tsp. grated or ground NUTMEG

Mix together:
1/4 cup BUTTER, room temperature
1 cup BROWN SUGAR
1 EGG, beaten
1 cup BUTTERMILK or YOGURT
1 Tbsp. grated ORANGE PEEL

Combine mixtures until just moist. Fold in:
1 cup grated CARROTS
1 cup chopped RAISINS or NUTS

Spoon into 2 sprayed 8 x 4 loaf pans. Bake at 350° for one hour.

Celery-Carrot-Nut Loaves

Combine:
1 cup FLOUR
1 cup WHEAT FLOUR
1/3 cup SUGAR
1/2 tsp. SALT
1 tsp. BAKING POWDER
1/2 tsp. BAKING SODA

Combine in order listed:
2 EGGS, beaten
1/3 cup MILK
1/3 cup SALAD OIL
1 cup grated CARROTS
1/2 cup finely chopped CELERY

Combine both mixtures until just moist then add:
2/3 cup chopped WALNUTS

Spoon into 2 sprayed 8 x 4 loaf pans. Bake at 350° for one hour.

Cereal Loaves

1/2 cup boiling WATER
1 cup GOLDEN RAISINS

Soak raisins in hot water for 20 minutes.

Combine:
2 cups FLOUR
1 Tbsp. BAKING POWDER
3 Tbsp. firmly packed BROWN SUGAR
1/2 tsp. CINNAMON

Mix together:
1 EGG, beaten
2 Tbsp. melted BUTTER
2/3 cup MILK
1 Tbsp. grated ORANGE PEEL

Combine all mixtures, stirring until just moistened then add the following:
1/2 cup chopped NUTS
3/4 cup nut-like CEREAL NUGGETS

Pour into sprayed 9 x 5 loaf pan. Bake at 375° for one hour.

Cheese-Apple Loaves

Cream until light and fluffy:
1/2 cup BUTTER, room temperature
2/3 cup SUGAR

Add one at a time, beating after each:
2 EGGS

Mix in:
1/2 cup grated or shredded CHEDDAR CHEESE
1 cup chopped APPLES
3/4 cup chopped NUTS

Sift together:
2 cups FLOUR
1 tsp. BAKING POWDER
1/2 tsp. BAKING SODA
1/2 tsp. SALT
1/4 tsp. NUTMEG

Combine mixtures until just moistened. Spoon evenly into sprayed 9 x 5 loaf pan. Bake at 350° for one hour.

Cheddar Cheese Loaves

Cream together:
>1/4 cup BUTTER, room temperature
>1/2 cup SUGAR

Beat in until light and fluffy:
>1 EGG
>2 tsp. grated ORANGE PEEL

Combine:
>2 cups FLOUR
>2 1/2 tsp. BAKING POWDER
>1/2 tsp. SALT

Add to creamed mixture alternately with:
>2/3 cup MILK

Fold in:
>1 cup GOLDEN RAISINS
>1 cup shredded or grated CHEDDAR CHEESE

Spoon into sprayed 9 x 5 loaf pan. Bake at 375° for 55 minutes.

Parmesan Loaves

Mix together in order listed:
>2 cups FLOUR
>1 tsp. SALT
>2 tsp. BAKING POWDER
>1 tsp. BAKING SODA
>1/8 tsp. CAYENNE
>1/2 tsp. SAGE
>1 tsp. PEPPER, coarse ground
>1 cup grated PARMESAN
>1/2 cup minced PARSLEY

Mix together:
>1/4 cup BUTTER, room temperature
>2 Tbsp. SUGAR
>1 cup BUTTERMILK
>1/2 tsp. WORCESTERSHIRE SAUCE

Combine mixtures until just moist. Spoon into 2 sprayed 8 x 4 loaf pans. Bake at 350° for one hour.

Cherry Loaves

Beat until creamy:
> **1/2 cup BUTTER, room temperature**
> **1/2 cup SUGAR**

Add one at a time:
> **2 EGGS**

Combine:
> **2 cups FLOUR**
> **2 tsp. BAKING POWDER**
> **1 tsp. grated ORANGE PEEL**
> **1/2 tsp. BAKING SODA**
> **1/2 tsp. SALT**

Add flour mixture alternately to batter with:
> **2/3 cup ORANGE JUICE**

Stir in:
> **2 cups drained and chopped CHERRIES, sweet dark**
> **1 tsp. VANILLA**
> **3/4 cup chopped PECANS or WALNUTS**

Pour into 2 sprayed 8 x 4 loaf pans. Bake at 350° for 50 minutes.

Chocolate Loaves

Sift together:
> **2 1/2 cups FLOUR**
> **1 1/2 tsp. BAKING SODA**
> **1/2 cup COCOA**
> **3/4 cup SUGAR**
> **1/2 tsp. SALT**

Combine:
> **1 EGG, beaten**
> **1/3 cup BUTTER, melted**
> **1 1/4 cups SOUR MILK**

This'll fix that sweet tooth!

Combine mixtures until just blended.

Fold in:
> **3/4 cup total of chopped ALMONDS, PECANS**
> **and/or WALNUTS**

Pour into sprayed 9 x 5 loaf pan. Bake at 350° for one hour.

Chocolate Chip Loaves

Sift together:
>1 cup FLOUR
>1/3 cup SUGAR
>1 tsp. BAKING SODA
>3/4 tsp. SALT

Stir in:
>1 cup QUICK OATS

Combine:
>1 EGG, lightly beaten
>1 tsp. VANILLA
>1 cup SOUR MILK
>1/4 cup SALAD OIL

Combine mixtures until just moist then stir in:
>1/2 cup CHOCOLATE CHIPS, MINIATURE
>1/2 cup chopped ALMONDS

Spoon into 2 sprayed 8 x 4 loaf pans. Bake at 325° for one hour and 10 minutes.

German Chocolate Loaves

Cream:
>1 cup BUTTER, room temperature
>3/4 cup SUGAR

Beat in well after each addition:
>3 EGGS
>1 EGG YOLK
>3/4 cup MILK
>1 tsp. VANILLA
>1 pkg. (4 oz.) GERMAN SWEET CHOCOLATE, melted

Combine and add:
>2 1/4 cups sifted FLOUR
>1 tsp. SALT
>1 1/2 tsp. BAKING SODA
>1/3 tsp. CINNAMON
>3/4 tsp. CREAM OF TARTAR

Stir in:
>1 cup chopped WALNUTS

Pour into sprayed 9 x 5 loaf pan. Bake at 350° for 55 minutes.

Chutney Loaves

Mix together:
> **1 3/4 cups FLOUR**
> **3/4 tsp. SALT**
> **1 tsp. BAKING SODA**
> **3/4 tsp. BAKING POWDER**
> **1 tsp. CINNAMON**
> **1/4 tsp. NUTMEG**

Combine in order shown:
> **1/3 cup BUTTER or MARGARINE, room temperature**
> **2/3 cup BROWN SUGAR**
> **2 EGGS, beaten**
> **1 cup puréed PUMPKIN**
> **1/4 cup MILK**
> **2/3 cup chopped CHUTNEY**
> **3/4 cup chopped NUTS**

Combine mixtures until just moistened and pour into 2 sprayed 8 x 4 loaf pans. Bake at 350° for one hour.

Cornmeal-Brown Bread Loaves

Mix together:
> **1 cup FLOUR**
> **1 cup WHEAT FLOUR**
> **1 1/2 tsp. BAKING SODA**
> **1 tsp. BAKING POWDER**
> **1/2 tsp. SALT**
> **1 cup CORNMEAL**

Combine:
> **3/4 cup MOLASSES**
> **2 cups SOUR MILK**

Combine mixtures.

Stir in:
> **1 1/2 cups RAISINS**

Fill 2 sprayed round cans half full or 3 sprayed 8 x 4 loaf pans. Bake at 350° for 50 minutes. Very good served hot. Excellent flavor, consistency and texture.

Cornmeal-Cheese-Onion Loaves

Mix together:
- 1 cup FLOUR
- 1/2 cup WHEAT FLOUR
- 1/2 cup YELLOW CORNMEAL
- 2 tsp. BAKING POWDER
- 1/2 tsp. SALT
- 1/2 tsp. DILL WEED

Mix together:
- 3 EGGS, beaten
- 3 Tbsp. HONEY
- 1/4 cup BUTTER, melted
- 1 cup MILK
- 1/4 cup minced ONION
- 1/2 cup chopped MILD GREEN CHILES
- 1 Tbsp. DIJON MUSTARD
- 3/4 cup shredded or grated CHEDDAR CHEESE

Combine mixtures until just moistened and pour into 3 sprayed 8 x 4 loaf pans. Bake at 350° for 50 minutes.

Cornmeal-Chile-Cheese Loaves

Mix together:
- 1 1/3 cups FLOUR
- 2/3 cup YELLOW CORNMEAL
- 1 Tbsp. BAKING POWDER
- 1 tsp. SALT

Combine in order listed:
- 3 EGGS, beaten
- 1/2 cup SALAD OIL
- 2 cups SOUR CREAM
- 3 Tbsp. chopped CHILE PEPPERS
- 1/3 cup chopped GREEN PEPPER
- 2 cups CREAMED CORN
- 1 cup grated CHEDDAR CHEESE

Combine mixtures until just moistened. Pour into sprayed 8" square baking dish. Bake at 350° for 45 minutes. Serve hot.

Cottage Cheese Loaves

Mix together:
- 2 cups FLOUR
- 1 Tbsp. BAKING POWDER
- 1/2 tsp. BAKING SODA
- 1/2 tsp. SALT
- 1 Tbsp. CARAWAY SEEDS

Cream:
- 1/3 cup BUTTER

Gradually add:
- 1/4 cup SUGAR

Add:
- 2 EGGS, beaten
- 1 cup COTTAGE CHEESE
- 1/2 cup MILK
- 1/2 cup RAISINS

Combine mixtures until moistened. Spoon into 3 sprayed 8 x 4 loaf pans. Bake at 350° for 50 minutes.

Cranberry-Date Loaves

Mix together:
- 2 cups FLOUR
- 2/3 cup SUGAR
- 1 tsp. BAKING SODA
- 1/2 tsp. SALT

Mix together:
- 2 EGGS, beaten
- 1 cup BUTTERMILK or YOGURT
- 3/4 cup SALAD OIL
- 1 Tbsp. grated ORANGE
    PEEL

Combine mixtures until just moist and stir in:
- 1 cup chopped DATES
- 1 1/2 cups sliced CRANBERRIES
- 1 cup chopped WALNUTS

Spoon into 4 sprayed 6 x 3 loaf pans. Bake at 350° for 50 minutes.

Cranberry-Orange Loaves

Mix together:
>   2 cups sifted FLOUR
>   2/3 cup SUGAR
>   2 tsp. BAKING POWDER
>   1/2 tsp. SALT
>   1/2 tsp. BAKING SODA

Combine:
>   1 EGG, beaten
>   3/4 cup ORANGE JUICE
>   2 tsp. grated ORANGE PEEL
>   1/4 cup SALAD OIL

Combine mixtures until moistened and fold in:
>   1/2 cup chopped PECANS or WALNUTS
>   1 1/2 cups sliced CRANBERRIES

*Spoon into 2 sprayed 8 x 4 loaf pans. Bake at 375° for one hour. This recipe also makes great **mini muffins** which bake in about 20 minutes.*

Cranberry-Relish Loaves

Mix together:
>   1 cup sifted WHEAT FLOUR
>   1 cup sifted FLOUR
>   3/4 cup SUGAR
>   1 Tbsp. BAKING POWDER
>   1 tsp. SALT
>   1/2 tsp. BAKING SODA
>   1/2 tsp. CINNAMON
>   1/4 tsp. NUTMEG

Combine:
>   1 EGG, beaten
>   2 Tbsp. SALAD OIL
>   1/2 cup ORANGE JUICE
>   1 Tbsp. grated ORANGE PEEL
>   1 cup drained WHOLE CRANBERRY SAUCE

Combine mixtures and stir in:
>   1/2 cup crushed WHEAT CEREAL
>   1/2 cup RAISINS

Pour into sprayed 9 x 5 loaf pan. Bake at 350° for one hour.

Cranberry-Walnut Loaves

Combine:
2 cups FLOUR
2 tsp. BAKING POWDER
1/2 tsp. BAKING SODA
1/2 tsp. SALT
2 Tbsp. SUGAR

Mix together:
1/4 cup BROWN SUGAR
1/2 cup chopped WALNUTS
1/2 tsp. CINNAMON

Add and beat:
1 EGG
2/3 cup MILK or WATER

Combine mixtures and stir in:
2/3 cup CRANBERRY SAUCE, WHOLE BERRIES

Pour into sprayed 9 x 5 loaf pan. Bake at 350° for one hour.

Date-Pumpkin Loaves

Cream:
    1/2 cup BUTTER, room temperature
    1 1/2 cups BROWN SUGAR

Add:
    1 cup PUMPKIN, cooked   4 EGG YOLKS
        or canned   1 1/2 tsp. VANILLA
    1/3 cup LOWFAT MILK

Combine and add:
    1 1/2 cups FLOUR   1/2 tsp. NUTMEG
    1 tsp. BAKING POWDER   1/2 tsp. BAKING SODA
    1 tsp. CINNAMON   1/2 tsp. GINGER
    1/2 tsp. SALT

Stir in:
    1 cup chopped PECANS or WALNUTS
    1 cup finely chopped DATES

Fold in:
    4 EGG WHITES, beaten until stiff.

Pour into 2 sprayed 8 x 4 loaf pans. Bake at 375° for one hour.

Date-Raisin Loaves

Combine:
    1 1/4 cups FLOUR
    1 tsp. BAKING POWDER
    1 tsp. BAKING SODA
    1/3 cup SUGAR
    1/4 tsp. SALT

Stir together until butter melted:
    2 Tbsp. BUTTER
    1/2 tsp. VANILLA
    1 cup hot WATER

Add:
    1 EGG, beaten   1/2 cup RAISINS
    1/2 tsp. CINNAMON   1/2 cup chopped WALNUTS
    8 oz. finely chopped DATES   or PECANS

Combine mixtures until just moistened and pour into 2 sprayed 8 x 4 loaf pans. Bake at 325° for one hour.

Eggnog Loaves

Sift together:
    3 cups FLOUR
    1/2 cup SUGAR
    1 Tbsp. BAKING POWDER
    1 tsp. SALT
    1/2 tsp. NUTMEG

Combine:
    1 1/2 cups EGGNOG
    1 EGG, beaten
    1/4 cup BUTTER, melted

Combine mixtures until just moistened.

Stir in:
    1 cup chopped WALNUTS or PECANS

Spoon into sprayed 9 x 5 loaf pan. Bake at 375° for one hour or more.

Fig Loaves

Combine, in order:
    1 1/2 cups chopped FIGS
    3/4 cup ORANGE JUICE
    2 Tbsp. BUTTER, melted
    1 EGG, beaten
    1 tsp. grated ORANGE PEEL
    1/2 cup chopped PECANS or WALNUTS

Mix together:
    2 cups FLOUR
    2 tsp. BAKING POWDER
    1/2 tsp. SALT
    1/3 cup SUGAR
    1/2 tsp. NUTMEG

Combine mixtures until just moistened and spoon into 2 sprayed 8 x 4 loaf pans. Bake at 375° for 50 minutes.

Fig-Apricot Loaves

Mix together:
- **1 cup FLOUR**
- **1 tsp. BAKING SODA**
- **1/2 tsp. SALT**
- **1 cup ROLLED OATS**

Combine, in order:
- **1 EGG, beaten until frothy**
- **1/2 cup BROWN SUGAR**
- **1/2 cup BUTTER, melted**
- **1 cup BUTTERMILK or YOGURT**

Combine mixtures until just moistened. Fold in:
- **1/2 cup chopped NUTS**
- **1/2 cup chopped FIGS**
- **1/2 cup chopped APRICOTS**
- **1 Tbsp. grated ORANGE PEEL**

Spoon into sprayed 9 x 5 loaf pan. Bake at 350° for one hour.

Dried Fruit Loaves

Simmer until water absorbed:
- **1/3 cup WATER**
- **1 1/2 cups chopped MIXED DRIED FRUITS**

Mix together:
- **2 cups FLOUR**
- **1/3 cup SUGAR**
- **1 Tbsp. BAKING POWDER**
- **3/4 tsp. SALT**
- **1/4 tsp. NUTMEG**

Combine and add to dried fruit mixture:
- **1 EGG, beaten**
- **1 cup MILK**
- **1/4 cup SALAD OIL**
- **3/4 cup chopped PECANS**

Combine mixtures until just moistened and spoon into 2 sprayed 8 x 4 loaf pans. Bake at 375° for 50 minutes.

Ginger Loaves

Cream:
> **1/2 cup BUTTER, room temperature**
> **1/3 cup SUGAR**

Add and beat until fluffy:
> **2 EGGS**
> **1 cup MILK**

Mix together:
> **2 cups sifted FLOUR**
> **1 3/4 tsp. GINGER**
> **1 1/4 tsp. CINNAMON**
> **1/4 tsp. GROUND CLOVES**
> **2 tsp. BAKING POWDER**
> **1/2 tsp. BAKING SODA**
> **1/2 tsp. SALT**

Combine mixtures until just moistened and spoon into sprayed 9 x 5 loaf pan. Bake at 350° for one hour.

Hickory Nut Loaves

Combine:
> **2 cups sifted FLOUR**
> **1/2 cup SUGAR**
> **1 Tbsp. BAKING POWDER**
> **1/2 tsp. SALT**
> **1/2 tsp. NUTMEG**

Combine:
> **1 EGG, beaten**
> **1 cup MILK**

Combine mixtures until just blended.

Stir in:
> **1 cup finely chopped HICKORY NUTS**

Pour into sprayed 9 x 5 loaf pan. Bake at 350° for 50 minutes.

Honey-Orange Loaves

Sift together:
   2 cups FLOUR
   1/2 tsp. BAKING SODA
   1/2 tsp. SALT
   2 1/2 tsp. BAKING POWDER

Cream:
   2 Tbsp. BUTTER
   1 cup HONEY

Add:
   1 EGG, beaten
   2/3 cup ORANGE JUICE

Combine mixtures until blended.

Fold in:
   3/4 cup chopped NUTS

Pour into sprayed 9 x 5 loaf pan. Bake at 350° for one hour 10 minutes.

Honey-Raisin Loaves

Mix together:
   2 cups FLOUR
   1 Tbsp. BAKING POWDER
   1/2 tsp. BAKING SODA
   1/2 tsp. SALT
   1/2 cup BRAN CEREAL, whole
   1/3 cup BROWN SUGAR

Combine:
   1 cup MILK
   2 EGGS, beaten
   1/3 cup HONEY
   3 Tbsp. BUTTER, melted

Combine mixtures until just blended and stir in:
   1 cup GOLDEN RAISINS
   3/4 cup chopped WALNUTS or PECANS

Pour into sprayed 8 x 4 loaf pans. Bake at 350° for one hour and 15 minutes.

Kiwi Loaves

Mix together:
1 1/2 cups FLOUR
1/2 tsp. BAKING POWDER
1/2 tsp. SALT
1/2 tsp. BAKING SODA
1/2 cup SUGAR

Combine:
1 cup peeled and chopped KIWI fruit
2 Tbsp. LEMON JUICE
1 EGG, beaten
1/2 cup SALAD OIL

Combine mixtures until ingredients are moistened. Spoon into sprayed 9 x 5 loaf pan. Bake at 350° for one hour.

Kumquat Loaves

Mix together:
2 cups FLOUR
1/2 cup SUGAR
1 tsp. BAKING SODA
1 tsp. SALT
1 Tbsp. BAKING POWDER
1/2 tsp. GINGER

Combine:
1 1/2 cups KUMQUAT PRESERVES*
1/2 cup BUTTER or MARGARINE, melted
2 Tbsp. LEMON JUICE

Fold in:
3/4 cup chopped PECANS
1 cup CREAM, whipped

*To make preserves, wash kumquats, chop and remove seeds, add 1 1/2 cup sugar, and cook uncovered until mixture cooks down a little and starts to thicken. Mixture will continue to thicken as it cools.

Spoon into 2 sprayed 8 x 4 loaf pans. Bake at 350° for 50 minutes.

Lemon Loaves

Cream until fluffy:
  1/2 cup BUTTER or MARGARINE, room temperature
  1 cup SUGAR

Add:
  2 EGG YOLKS
  2/3 cup MILK

Sift together:
  2 cups FLOUR
  1/2 tsp. SALT
  1 tsp. BAKING POWDER

Combine mixtures until just moistened and stir in:
  1/2 cup finely chopped PECANS
  2 tsp. grated LEMON PEEL

Fold in:
  2 EGG WHITES, stiffly beaten

Pour into 2 sprayed 8 x 4 loaf pans. Bake at 350° for one hour.

Lemon Topping

Pour mixture over bread as soon as it comes out of oven:
  2 tsp. LEMON JUICE
  2 Tbsp. SUGAR

Lemon-Lime Loaves

Cream:
>   1/2 cup BUTTER or MARGARINE, room temperature
>   3/4 cup SUGAR

Add:
>   2 EGGS, beaten
>   1/4 cup LEMON JUICE
>   1/4 cup LIME JUICE

Combine:
>   1 1/3 cup FLOUR
>   1 tsp. BAKING POWDER
>   1/2 tsp. SALT

Combine mixtures until just moistened and stir in:
>   3/4 cup chopped CASHEWS
>   1 grated LEMON PEEL
>   1 grated LIME PEEL

Pour into sprayed 9 x 5 loaf pan. Bake at 350° for one hour.

Lettuce Loaves

Mix together:
>   1 1/2 cups FLOUR
>   2 tsp. BAKING POWDER
>   1/2 tsp. BAKING SODA
>   1/2 tsp. SALT
>   1/4 tsp. NUTMEG
>   1/8 tsp. GINGER
>   3/4 cup SUGAR

Combine:
>   2 EGGS, beaten
>   1/2 cup SALAD OIL
>   1 1/2 tsp. grated LEMON PEEL

Combine mixtures until just moist and stir in:
>   1 cup finely chopped LETTUCE
>   2/3 cup chopped NUTS

Spoon into sprayed 8 x 4 loaf pan. Bake at 350° for 55 minutes.

Maple Syrup Loaves

Mix together:
   1 cup WHEAT FLOUR
   1 1/2 cups FLOUR
   1 tsp. BAKING POWDER
   1 tsp. BAKING SODA

Combine:
   1 1/2 cups BUTTERMILK
   1/2 cup MAPLE SYRUP
   1 EGG, beaten
   1 1/2 Tbsp. BUTTER, melted

Combine mixtures until just moistened and stir in:
   1 cup GOLDEN RAISINS, plumped*

*Covered with hot water for 10 minutes and drained.

Pour into sprayed 9 x 5 loaf pan. Bake at 350° for 50 minutes.

Mincemeat Loaves

Sift together:
   3 cups FLOUR
   1 Tbsp. BAKING POWDER
   1 tsp. SALT
   1/4 cup SUGAR

Mix together:
   1 cup mashed BANANA
   1/2 cup CORN SYRUP
   1/2 cup ORANGE JUICE
   1/4 cup SALAD OIL
   1 EGG, beaten
   1 cup MINCEMEAT
   1/4 cup BRANDY

*Combine mixtures until just moistened and spoon into 3 sprayed
8 x 4 loaf pans. Bake at 350° for one hour.*

Molasses Loaves

Sift together:
1 1/2 cups FLOUR
1/2 cup WHEAT FLOUR
1/2 cup SUGAR
1/2 tsp. BAKING POWDER
1/2 tsp. BAKING SODA
1/4 tsp. CINNAMON
1/4 tsp. NUTMEG
1/4 tsp. GINGER

Beat together:
1/2 cup MOLASSES, unsulphured
1/4 cup SALAD OIL

Combine mixtures until just moistened and stir in:
1 cup chopped PECANS

Pour into 2 sprayed 8 x 4 loaf pans. Bake at 350° for 35 minutes.

Nut Loaves

Sift together:
2 cups FLOUR
1 Tbsp. BAKING POWDER
1/2 tsp. SALT
1/3 cup SUGAR

Combine:
1 EGG, beaten
1 cup MILK
2 Tbsp. BUTTER or MARGARINE, melted

Combine mixtures until just moistened and stir in:
3/4 cup finely chopped NUTS.

Spoon into 9 x 5 sprayed loaf pan. Bake at 375° for one hour.

Oatmeal-Brandy Loaves

Combine:
    1 cup OATS, quick
    1 1/2 cups WATER, boiling

Cream:
    1/2 cup BUTTER or MARGARINE, room temperature
    1/2 cup SUGAR
    3/4 cup BROWN SUGAR

Sift together:
    2 cups FLOUR
    1 tsp. SALT
    1 tsp. BAKING POWDER
    1 tsp. BAKING SODA
    1 tsp. CINNAMON
    1 tsp. NUTMEG
    1 tsp. GROUND CLOVES
    1/2 tsp. GINGER

Add:
    3 EGGS, one at a time
    1 tsp. VANILLA
    2 Tbsp. BRANDY or DARK RUM
    1 cup APPLESAUCE

Combine all mixtures until just moistened and stir in:
    1 cup RAISINS
    1 cup chopped WALNUTS

Spoon into sprayed 9 x 5 loaf pan. Bake at 350° for one hour 20 minutes.

Oat Loaves

Mix together:
1 cup FLOUR
3/4 cup WHEAT FLOUR
2 tsp. BAKING POWDER
1/2 tsp. BAKING SODA
1/2 tsp. SALT

Mix together:
2 EGGS, beaten
2 Tbsp. SALAD OIL
1/4 cup HONEY
1/2 cup BROWN SUGAR
1 cup MILK or BUTTERMILK or YOGURT

Spread out on baking sheet. Toast at 350° 15 to 20 minutes:
1 cup ROLLED OATS
3 Tbsp. WHEAT GERM

Combine all mixtures until just moistened and pour into sprayed 9 x 5 loaf pan. Bake at 375° for one hour.

Oat-Banana Loaves

Mix together:
1 cup FLOUR
1/3 cup WHEAT FLOUR
1/2 cup ROLLED OATS
1 tsp. BAKING POWDER
1/2 tsp. SALT
1 tsp. NUTMEG

Cream:
1/2 cup BUTTER, room temperature
1/2 cup HONEY

Add to creamed mixture:
2 EGGS, one at a time
1/2 tsp. VANILLA
1 cup mashed BANANA
3/4 cup chopped NUTS

Combine all mixtures until just moistened and spoon into sprayed 6 x 3 loaf pans. Bake at 350° for 45 minutes.

Oat-Lemon Loaves

Cream together:
>3 Tbsp. BUTTER or MARGARINE, room temperature
>3/4 cup SUGAR

Add and beat until smooth:
>2 EGGS

Add:
>2 cups MILK

Sift together:
>2 cups FLOUR
>1 Tbsp. BAKING POWDER
>1/2 tsp. SALT

Combine:
>1 cup ROLLED OATS
>1 cup chopped NUTS
>2 tsp. grated LEMON PEEL

Combine all mixtures until just moistened and pour into sprayed 8 x 4 loaf pans. Bake at 350° for 45 to 55 minutes.

Oat-Molasses Loaves

Spread on baking sheet:
>1 1/4 cups ROLLED OATS
>1/2 cup chopped NUTS

Bake at 350° for 20 minutes:

Mix together:
>1 cup FLOUR
>1 cup WHEAT FLOUR
>1 tsp. BAKING POWDER
>1 tsp. BAKING SODA
>1/2 tsp. SALT
>1/4 cup SUGAR

Mix together:
>2 EGGS, beaten
>1/3 cup MOLASSES
>2 Tbsp. BUTTER, melted
>1 cup MILK or BUTTERMILK or YOGURT

Combine all mixtures until just moistened. Spoon into 2 sprayed 8 x 4 loaf pans. Bake at 350° for 50 to 60 minutes.

Olive-Spinach Loaves

Thaw and squeeze dry:
   1 box (10 oz.) FROZEN CHOPPED SPINACH

Combine with:
   1/2 cup chopped RIPE OLIVES
   1/2 cup SOUR CREAM
   1/2 cup MILK
   1/3 cup grated CHEDDAR CHEESE
   2 Tbsp. BUTTER, melted

Mix together:
   1 cup FLOUR
   1 Tbsp. BAKING POWDER
   1 Tbsp. SUGAR
   1/2 tsp. BAKING SODA
   1/2 tsp. SALT
   1/4 tsp. NUTMEG

Combine mixtures until just moistened and spoon into 2 sprayed 8 x 4 loaf pans. Bake at 375° for 40 to 50 minutes.

Onion-Caraway Loaves

Mix together:
   1 1/4 cups FLOUR
   1 tsp. BAKING POWDER
   3/4 tsp. BAKING SODA
   1/2 tsp. SALT
   1 Tbsp. CARAWAY SEEDS

Sauté:
   1/2 cup BUTTER, melted
   1/2 cup finely chopped ONION

Remove from heat.

Add:
   1 cup BRAN CEREAL
   1 cup BUTTERMILK or YOGURT

Beat in:
   1 EGG

Combine mixtures until just moistened and pour into 2 sprayed 8 x 4 loaf pans. Bake at 350° for 45 to 55 minutes.

Onion-Eggplant Loaves

Mix together:
>1 1/2 cups FLOUR
>1 Tbsp. BAKING POWDER
>1/2 tsp. SALT

Combine:
>2 EGGS, beaten
>1/2 cup SALAD OIL
>1/2 cup MILK
>1/2 cup grated or shredded CHEDDAR CHEESE
>1 cup finely chopped EGGPLANT
>1 Tbsp. minced ONION

Combine mixtures until just moistened.

Stir in:
>1 cup BRAN KERNEL CEREAL

Spoon into 2 sprayed 6 x 3 loaf pans. Bake at 350° for one hour.

Onion-Olive Loaves

Mix together:
>2 cups FLOUR
>2 tsp. BAKING POWDER
>1/2 tsp. BAKING SODA
>1/2 tsp. SALT
>4 Tbsp. BUTTERMILK POWDER
>1/3 cup MASHED POTATO FLAKES
>3 Tbsp. minced ONION

Mix together:
>1 cup grated MONTEREY JACK CHEESE
>3/4 cup MILK
>1/2 cup SOUR CREAM
>2 Tbsp. BUTTER, melted
>1 EGG, beaten
>1/2 cup chopped RIPE OLIVES

*Combine mixtures until just moistened and spoon into sprayed
9 x 5 loaf pan. Bake at 350° for 55 minutes.*

Orange Loaves

Blend:
- 1 EGG, beaten
- 1 Tbsp. grated ORANGE PEEL
- 2/3 cup ORANGE JUICE

Sift together:
- 2 cups FLOUR
- 1 tsp. BAKING POWDER
- 1 tsp. BAKING SODA
- 1/2 tsp. SALT
- 2 Tbsp. SUGAR

Combine mixtures until just moistened and pour into a sprayed 9 x 5 loaf pan. Bake at 350° for one hour.

Orange Topping

- 1/2 cup POWDERED SUGAR
- 1 tsp. grated ORANGE PEEL
- 2 tsp. ORANGE JUICE

Drizzle over bread hot out of the oven.

Orange-Banana-Date Loaves

Combine in order given:
- 2 cups FLOUR
- 1 tsp. BAKING POWDER
- 1 tsp. BAKING SODA
- 1/2 tsp. SALT
- 1/3 cup SUGAR
- 2 EGGS, beaten
- 1 Tbsp. grated ORANGE PEEL
- 1/2 cup ORANGE JUICE
- 8 oz. pkg. DATES, chopped
- 1 cup mashed BANANAS

Pour into sprayed 9 x 5 loaf pan. Bake at 350° for one hour.

Orange Liqueur Loaves

Cream until fluffy:
1 cup BUTTER, room temperature
1/2 cup SUGAR

Beat in one at a time:
3 EGG YOLKS
1 tsp. ORANGE LIQUEUR

Sift together:
2 cups FLOUR
1 tsp. BAKING POWDER
1 tsp. BAKING SODA

Add flour mixture to batter alternately with:
1 1/4 cups SOUR CREAM

Stir in:
Grated rind of one ORANGE
1 cup chopped WALNUTS or PECANS

Fold in:
3 EGG WHITES, stiffly beaten

Spoon into sprayed 9 x 5 loaf pan. Bake at 350° for 50 to 60 minutes.

Orange Liqueur Topping

1/4 cup SUGAR
1/2 cup ORANGE JUICE
2 1/2 Tbsp. ORANGE LIQUEUR
1/2 cup toasted ALMONDS

Combine ingredients and pour over bread hot out of the oven. Allow to cool before removing.

Orange Marmalade Loaves

Mix together:
- **2 cups FLOUR**
- **1/2 cup WHEAT FLOUR**
- **1 Tbsp. BAKING POWDER**
- **1 tsp. SALT**
- **1/2 tsp. BAKING SODA**

Combine:
- **1/2 cup BROWN SUGAR**
- **1/3 cup SALAD OIL**
- **1 EGG, beaten**
- **1 cup ORANGE MARMALADE**
- **3/4 cup ORANGE JUICE**
- **1 tsp. grated LEMON PEEL**

Combine mixtures until just blended.

Stir in:
- **1 cup chopped NUTS**

Pour into two sprayed 8 x 4 loaf pans. Bake at 350° for 50 to 60 minutes.

Orange Marmalade Topping

While loaf is still warm, pierce top and cover with:
- **1/4 cup ORANGE MARMALADE, warmed**

Orange-Plum Loaves

Cream until fluffy:
1/2 cup BUTTER or MARGARINE, room temperature

Add:
2 Tbsp. SUGAR
3/4 tsp. VANILLA
1/4 tsp. LEMON EXTRACT
2 EGGS, add one at a time

Mix together:
1 1/2 cup FLOUR
1/2 tsp. SALT
1/2 tsp. CREAM OF TARTAR
1/2 tsp. BAKING SODA
1 tsp. BAKING POWDER

In stainless saucepan, bring to boil and simmer until fruit is clear:
10 PLUMS, halved and seeded
3/4 cup SUGAR

Cool and add:
1/3 cup ORANGE JUICE

Combine all mixtures until just moistened and stir in:
1 cup chopped WALNUTS

Spoon into 2 sprayed 8 x 4 loaf pans. Bake at 350° for 45 minutes.

Orange-Raisin Loaves

Mix together:
2 cups FLOUR
1 tsp. BAKING SODA
1/2 tsp. SALT
3/4 cup SUGAR

Combine:
2 EGGS, beaten
1/2 cup BUTTER, melted
3/4 cup BUTTERMILK or YOGURT

Combine mixtures until just moistened then add:
1 cup chopped RAISINS
Grated peel of 3 large ORANGES
1/2 cup chopped WALNUTS

Pour into sprayed 9 x 5 loaf pan. Bake at 350° for 50 to 60 minutes.

Peach Loaves

Mix together:
2 cups FLOUR
2 tsp. BAKING POWDER
1/2 tsp. BAKING SODA
1/2 tsp. SALT
1/2 tsp. CINNAMON
1/4 tsp. NUTMEG

Combine:
1 EGG, beaten
1 cup BUTTERMILK or YOGURT*
2 Tbsp. BUTTER, melted
1 Tbsp. grated ORANGE PEEL
1 1/2 cups mashed PEACHES or NECTARINES,
**   sprinkled with LEMON JUICE**
1 cup BROWN SUGAR

Combine mixtures until just moistened and stir in:
1 1/2 cups chopped PECANS or WALNUTS

Or 6 Tbsp. POWDERED BUTTERMILK *and* **1 cup WATER.** *Spoon into 2 sprayed 8 x 4 loaf pans. Bake at 350° for 50 to 60 minutes.*

Peanut Loaves

Mix together:
2 cups FLOUR, sifted
2 tsp. BAKING POWDER
1/2 tsp. SALT
3/4 cup SUGAR

Combine:
2 EGGS, beaten
1/2 cup BUTTER, melted
1 tsp. VANILLA
1/2 cup MILK

Combine mixtures until just moistened and stir in:
3/4 cup chopped PEANUTS

Pour into sprayed 9 x 5 loaf pan. Bake at 350° for one hour.

Try these toppings:
- **1/3 cup PEANUT BUTTER**
- **1/3 cup CURRANT JELLY, thinned with WATER**

Peanut Butter Loaves

Mix together:
2 cups FLOUR
1/4 cup SUGAR
1/4 cup BROWN SUGAR
2 tsp. BAKING POWDER
1/2 tsp. BAKING SODA
1 tsp. SALT

Combine:
1 EGG, beaten
1 cup MILK
3/4 cup CHUNKY PEANUT BUTTER

Combine mixtures until just moistened and spoon into sprayed 9 x 5 loaf pan. Bake at 350° for 45 to 50 minutes.

Peanut Butter-Banana Loaves

Mix together:
2 cups FLOUR
1 1/2 tsp. BAKING POWDER
1/2 tsp. SALT
1/2 tsp. CINNAMON
1/4 tsp. BAKING SODA

Combine:
1/4 cup MARGARINE or BUTTER, room temperature
1/3 cup CHUNKY PEANUT BUTTER
1/3 cup BROWN SUGAR
1 EGG, beaten
1/4 cup MOLASSES
1/2 cup MILK

Combine mixtures until just moistened and fold in:
1 1/2 cups mashed BANANAS
1 cup chopped PEANUTS or PECANS

Spoon into sprayed 9 x 5 loaf pan. Bake at 350° for one hour.

Pear Loaves

Mix together:
2 cups FLOUR
1 tsp. BAKING POWDER
1/2 tsp. BAKING SODA
1/4 tsp. SALT
3/4 cup SUGAR
1 tsp. CINNAMON
1/4 tsp. NUTMEG

Combine:
2 EGGS, beaten
1/2 cup BUTTER, melted
1/2 cup BUTTERMILK or YOGURT
1 cup chopped PEARS

Combine mixtures until just moistened and stir in:
1 cup chopped ALMONDS

Pour into sprayed 9 x 5 loaf pan. Bake at 350° for one hour.

Pecan Loaves

Combine:
>   1 EGG, beaten until frothy
>   1 cup BROWN SUGAR, add a little at a time
>   1 Tbsp. BUTTER, melted
>   2 cups SOUR MILK

Mix together:
>   2 cups FLOUR
>   1 tsp. BAKING POWDER
>   1/2 tsp. SALT
>   1/2 tsp. BAKING SODA
>   1/4 tsp. NUTMEG
>   1/4 tsp. CINNAMON

Combine mixtures until just moistened and stir in:
>   1 1/2 cups chopped PECANS

Pour into sprayed 9 x 5 loaf pan. Bake at 350° for 50 to 55 minutes.

Persimmon Loaves

Combine in order given:
>   1/2 cup MARGARINE, melted
>   1 cup BROWN SUGAR
>   2 EGGS
>   1 cup peeled and mashed PERSIMMONS
>   1/4 cup WATER

Mix together:
>   2 cups FLOUR
>   1 tsp. SALT
>   1/4 tsp. GROUND CLOVES
>   1/4 tsp. ALLSPICE
>   1 tsp. BAKING SODA
>   1/2 tsp. BAKING POWDER

Combine mixtures until just moistened and stir in:
>   1/2 cup RAISINS
>   1/2 cup chopped PECANS

Spoon into 2 sprayed 8 x 4 loaf pans. Bake at 350° for one hour.

Pineapple Loaves

Combine:
1/2 cup crushed PINEAPPLE
2/3 cup BRAN CEREAL or CEREAL WITH DRIED
    FRUITS AND NUTS
2/3 cup PINEAPPLE SYRUP or JUICE
1 EGG, beaten
2 Tbsp. BUTTER, melted

Mix together:
2 cups FLOUR
2 tsp. BAKING POWDER
1/2 tsp. BAKING SODA
1/2 tsp. SALT
1/3 cup SUGAR

Combine mixtures until just moistened and stir in:
3/4 cup chopped ALMONDS or MACADAMIA NUTS

Pour into sprayed 9 x 5 loaf pan. Bake at 350° for one hour 10 minutes.

Poppy Seed Loaves

Combine and soak for 15 minutes:
1/3 cup POPPY SEEDS
1 cup BUTTERMILK

Mix together:
2 1/3 cups FLOUR
1 tsp. BAKING POWDER
1/2 tsp. BAKING SODA
1/4 tsp. SALT
3/4 cup SUGAR

Combine:
2 EGG YOLKS, beaten until light
1/4 cup BUTTER or MARGARINE, melted
1 tsp. ALMOND FLAVORING

Combine mixtures until just moistened and fold in:
2 EGG WHITES, beaten until stiff.

Spoon into sprayed 9 x 5 loaf pan. Bake at 350° for one hour.

Prune Loaves

Mix together in order listed:
3 EGGS, beaten
3/4 cup SALAD OIL
1/2 cup SUGAR
3/4 cup BROWN SUGAR
1 cup BUTTERMILK
1 1/2 tsp. BAKING SODA,
dissolved in buttermilk
1 tsp. ALLSPICE
1/2 tsp. VANILLA
2 cups FLOUR
1 cup cooked and chopped
PRUNES
1 cup chopped WALNUTS
or PECANS

Pour into sprayed 9 x 5 loaf pan. Bake at 350° for one hour.

Pumpkin Loaves

Mix together:
2 cups FLOUR
1 1/2 cup BROWN SUGAR
1 tsp. BAKING SODA
3/4 tsp. SALT
1/2 tsp. CINNAMON
1/2 tsp. NUTMEG
1/4 tsp. GROUND CLOVES

Combine:
2 EGGS, beaten
1/2 cup SALAD OIL
1/4 cup WATER
1 cup puréed or canned PUMPKIN

Combine mixtures until just moistened and stir in:
1 cup chopped PECANS

Pour into sprayed 9 x 5 loaf pan. Bake at 350° for one hour.

Pumpkin-Apple Loaves

Mix together:
>**2 cups FLOUR**
>**1 Tbsp. BAKING POWDER**
>**1/2 tsp. BAKING SODA**
>**1/2 tsp. SALT**
>**1/2 tsp. CINNAMON**
>**1/2 tsp. grated NUTMEG**
>**1/4 tsp. GROUND CLOVES**
>**1/4 tsp. GINGER**

Combine:
>**2 EGGS, beaten**
>**3/4 cup SUGAR**
>**1/2 cup BUTTER, melted**
>**1 cup canned or puréed PUMPKIN**
>**1 1/2 cups chopped TART APPLES**

Combine mixtures until just moistened and pour into 3 sprayed 8 x 4 loaf pans. Bake at 350° for 50 minutes.

Pumpkin-Ginger Loaves

Mix together:
>**2 1/2 cups FLOUR**
>**1/2 cup WHEAT GERM**
>**2 Tbsp. BAKING POWDER**
>**1/2 tsp. BAKING SODA**
>**1 tsp. SALT**
>**1 tsp. CINNAMON**
>**1/2 tsp. GINGER**
>**1/4 tsp. NUTMEG**

Beat together:
>**3/4 cup SUGAR**
>**1/2 cup SALAD OIL**
>**2 EGGS, beaten**
>**2 cups puréed or canned PUMPKIN**

Combine mixtures until just moistened and pour into 2 sprayed 8 x 4 loaf pans. Bake at 375° for 45 minutes.

Pumpkin-Molasses Loaves

Cream:
> 1/2 cup BUTTER or MARGARINE, room temperature
> 1 cup BROWN SUGAR

Beat in:
> 2 EGGS, one at a time
> 1/2 cup MOLASSES
> 1 1/4 cups canned or puréed PUMPKIN

Mix together:

2 1/4 cups FLOUR	1 tsp. CINNAMON
1/2 tsp. BAKING POWDER	1/2 tsp. GINGER
1 tsp. BAKING SODA	1/2 tsp. NUTMEG
1/2 tsp. SALT	

Combine mixtures until just moistened and stir in:
> 1 cup chopped WALNUTS
> 1/3 cup RAISINS

Pour into sprayed 9 x 5 loaf pan. Bake at 350° for one hour.

Pumpkin-Raisin Loaves

Cream:
> 1/3 cup BUTTER, room temperature
> 3/4 cup SUGAR
> 1/3 cup BROWN SUGAR

Combine and add to butter:
> 2 EGGS, beaten
> 1/4 cup WATER
> 1 cup canned or puréed PUMPKIN

Sift together:

1 3/4 cups FLOUR	1/2 tsp. BAKING POWDER
1 tsp. BAKING SODA	1/2 tsp. CINNAMON
3/4 tsp. SALT	1/2 tsp. GROUND CLOVES

Add dry ingredients 1/3 at a time to batter and stir in:
> 1/2 cup chopped NUTS
> 1 cup chopped RAISINS

Spoon into sprayed 9 x 5 loaf pan. Bake at 350° for one hour.

Raisin-Almond Loaves

Combine:
> 1 cup WATER, boiling
> 3/4 cup RAISINS

Mix together:
> 2/3 cup BROWN SUGAR
> 1/3 cup SALAD OIL
> 1/3 cup MOLASSES
> 1 EGG, beaten

Mix together:
> 2 cups FLOUR
> 1 1/2 tsp. BAKING SODA
> 3/4 tsp. NUTMEG
> 1/2 tsp. SALT

Combine mixtures until just moistened and fold in:
> 3/4 cup chopped ALMONDS

Spoon into sprayed 9 x 5 loaf pan. Bake at 350° for one hour.

Raisin-Bran Loaves

Combine and let stand:
> 1 cup WHOLE BRAN CEREAL
> 3/4 cup WATER

Beat until fluffy:
> 1/2 cup BUTTER or MARGARINE, room temperature
> 1/2 cup SUGAR

Add to creamed mixture:
> 2 EGGS, beaten
> 1/4 cup BROWN SUGAR

Mix together:
> 1 cup FLOUR, sifted
> 2 1/2 tsp. BAKING POWDER
> 1/2 tsp. SALT
> 1 tsp. CINNAMON

Combine mixtures until just moistened and stir in:
> 1 cup RAISINS
> 1 cup chopped NUTS

Pour into sprayed 9 x 5 loaf pan. Bake at 350° for one hour.

Raspberry Loaves

Cream:
1/2 cup BUTTER, room temperature
1/2 cup SUGAR

Add and beat until fluffy:
2 EGGS, one at a time

Add:
1/3 cup SOUR CREAM or YOGURT

Mix together:
2 cups FLOUR
1 tsp. BAKING POWDER
1/2 tsp. BAKING SODA
1/2 tsp. SALT

Combine mixtures until just moistened and gently fold in:
1 cup RASPBERRIES
1/2 cup chopped NUTS

Spoon into 2 sprayed 8 x 4 loaf pans. Bake at 350° for 40 to 50 minutes.

Rhubarb Loaves

Combine in order given:
1/2 cup SUGAR
1 cup BROWN SUGAR
1/2 cup SALAD OIL
1 1/4 cups BUTTERMILK or YOGURT
1 tsp. CINNAMON
1 tsp. BAKING SODA
1 tsp. SALT
1 tsp. VANILLA
1 EGG, beaten
2 1/2 cups FLOUR
1 1/2 cups finely chopped RHUBARB
3/4 cup chopped PECANS or WALNUTS

Mix until just moistened. Spoon into a sprayed 9 x 5 loaf pan and a sprayed 8 x 4 loaf pan. Bake at 350° for 50 to 55 minutes for smaller loaf, one hour for larger loaf.

(Irish) Soda Loaves

Sift together:
2 cups FLOUR, sifted
1 1/2 tsp. BAKING SODA
1/2 tsp. SALT
2 Tbsp. SUGAR

Cut in:
1/2 cup chilled SHORTENING

Stir in:
1 cup RAISINS
1 Tbsp. CARAWAY SEEDS

Combine:
2 EGGS, beaten
3/4 cup BUTTERMILK

Gradually add to flour mixture. Knead briefly and shape into loaf. Put in 9 x 5 sprayed loaf pan. Brush top with milk. Make criss-cross slashes on top. Bake at 375° for 40 to 50 minutes.

Squash Loaves

Sift together:
2 cups FLOUR
1 Tbsp. BAKING POWDER
1 tsp. SALT
1/4 tsp. CINNAMON
1/4 tsp. GINGER
1/8 tsp. GROUND CLOVES
1/4 cup SUGAR
1/2 cup BROWN SUGAR

Heat until butter softened:
3/4 cup MILK
2 Tbsp. BUTTER

Beat in:
1 cup cooked and mashed BUTTERNUT SQUASH
1 EGG

Combine mixtures until just moistened and fold in:
1/2 cup chopped NUTS
1/3 cup RAISINS

Pour into sprayed 9 x 5 loaf pan. Bake at 350° for one hour.

Strawberry Loaves

Sift together:
>   3 cups FLOUR, sifted
>   1 tsp. SALT
>   1/2 tsp. BAKING SODA
>   1 tsp. CREAM OF TARTAR
>   1 tsp. BAKING POWDER

Cream until fluffy:
>   1 cup BUTTER, room temperature
>   1 cup SUGAR
>   1 tsp. VANILLA
>   1/2 tsp. LEMON EXTRACT

Add one at a time:
>   4 EGGS

Combine:
>   1 1/4 cups STRAWBERRY JAM or PRESERVES
>   2/3 cup SOUR CREAM or YOGURT

Combine all mixtures until just moistened and stir in:
>   1 cup chopped WALNUTS or PECANS

Pour into 3 sprayed 8 x 4 loaf pans. Bake at 350° for 50 minutes.

Sweet Potato Loaves

Combine:
>   1 1/2 cups mashed SWEET POTATOES
>   1/2 cup BUTTER, melted
>   3 Tbsp. SUGAR
>   1 tsp. NUTMEG
>   1 tsp. ALLSPICE
>   1/2 tsp. CINNAMON
>   2 cups FLOUR, sifted
>   1 tsp. BAKING POWDER
>   1/2 tsp. BAKING SODA
>   1/2 tsp. SALT
>   2 EGGS, beaten

Pour into sprayed 9 x 5 loaf pan. Bake at 350° for one hour.

Vitamin Loaves

Combine in order given:
2 cups FLOUR
1 tsp. BAKING POWDER
1 tsp. BAKING SODA
1/2 tsp. SALT
2 Tbsp. SUGAR
1 EGG, beaten
2/3 cup MILK

Fold in:
1 1/2 cups VITAMIN PACKED CEREAL

Spoon into sprayed 9 x 5 loaf pan. Bake at 350° for one hour.

Wheat-Apricot-Prune Loaves

Mix together:
2 cups BUCKWHEAT FLOUR or (1 3/4 cups WHEAT
FLOUR plus 1/4 cup WHEAT GERM, toasted)
3/4 tsp. SALT
1/2 tsp. BAKING POWDER
1 1/2 tsp. BAKING SODA

Combine:
1 1/2 cups BUTTERMILK or YOGURT
1/2 cup BROWN SUGAR

Combine mixtures until just moistened and stir in:
1/2 cup chopped DRIED APRICOTS
1/2 cup soaked, drained and chopped DRIED PRUNES
1/2 cup RAISINS

Spoon into sprayed 9 x 5 loaf pan. Bake at 350° for 50 to 60 minutes.

Wheat-Walnut Loaves

Sift together:
2 cups WHEAT FLOUR, sifted
1 Tbsp. BAKING POWDER
1/2 tsp. SALT
1/2 cup BROWN SUGAR

Cut in:
1/3 cup cold BUTTER or MARGARINE

Add:
1 EGG, beaten
1 cup MILK

Fold in:
1 cup chopped WALNUTS
1/2 cup chopped DATES

Stir until blended. Spoon into sprayed 9 x 5 loaf pan. Bake at 350° for one hour.

Whiskey Loaves

Cream:
1 cup BUTTER, room temperature
1/2 cup SUGAR

Add:
2 EGGS, beaten
1/2 cup SCOTCH WHISKEY

Mix together:
2 cups FLOUR
1 tsp. BAKING SODA
1/2 tsp. SALT
2 tsp. grated LEMON PEEL

Combine mixtures until just moistened and stir in:
1/2 cup RAISINS
1/2 cup chopped NUTS

Spoon into sprayed 9 x 5 loaf pan. Bake at 350° for one hour.

Yogurt-Citrus Loaves

Cream:
1/2 cup BUTTER, room temperature
1 cup BROWN SUGAR

Beat in:
1 tsp. grated ORANGE PEEL or LEMON PEEL
1 tsp. VANILLA

Add and beat in one at a time:
3 EGGS

Add:
1 cup YOGURT

Mix together:
2 cups FLOUR
1/2 tsp. BAKING SODA
1/2 tsp. SALT

Combine mixtures until just moistened and stir in:
1/2 cup chopped PECANS or GRANOLA

Spoon into sprayed 9 x 5 loaf pan. Bake at 350° for 50 to 60 minutes.

Now that's a LOAF!

Yogurt-Raisin Loaves

Sift together:
    1 1/2 cups WHEAT FLOUR
    1/4 cup WHEAT GERM, toasted
    3/4 cup SUGAR
    2 tsp. BAKING POWDER
    1/2 tsp. SALT

Combine:
    1 cup YOGURT, flavored or unflavored
    1/2 cup SALAD OIL
    2 EGGS, beaten
    1 tsp. grated ORANGE or LEMON PEEL

Combine mixtures and stir in:
    1/2 cup chopped PECANS
    1/2 cup RAISINS

Spoon into sprayed 8 x 4 loaf pan. Put the following topping on loaf before or after baking. Bake at 350° for 50 to 60 minutes.

Butter-Cinnamon Topping

Combine:
    3 Tbsp. BUTTER, melted
    2 Tbsp. BROWN SUGAR
    1/2 tsp. CINNAMON
    3/4 cup chopped NUTS

Put on hot loaf just before baking or when hot out of the oven.

Zucchini Loaves

Beat:
    3 EGGS, until fluffy

Add and blend well:
    1 3/4 cups SUGAR
    1 cup SALAD OIL
    2 3/4 tsp. VANILLA

Stir in:
    2 cups unpeeled, grated ZUCCHINI

Combine and add to batter:
    3 cups FLOUR
    1 1/2 tsp. BAKING POWDER
    2 tsp. BAKING SODA
    1 tsp. SALT
    3 tsp. CINNAMON

Fold in:
    1 cup chopped PECANS

Pour into 3 sprayed 8 x 4 loaf pans. Bake at 350° for one hour. This bread has an unusual flavor, somewhat delicate and quite good. Excellent at room temperature. Rave reviews for this one!

Flavored Butters

Beat until fluffy:

   1/2 cup BUTTER or MARGARINE, room temperature

Combine with any one of the following:

Chives - Parsley

2 Tbsp. minced PARSLEY
1 tsp. LEMON JUICE
2 Tbsp. SOUR CREAM
1 tsp. CHIVES

PARSLEY

Dill

1 1/2 Tbsp. DILL SEED or DILL WEED
2 hard-cooked EGG YOLKS, strained
PEPPER, a sprinkling

DILL

Fruit

1/4 cup JAM or PRESERVES or
   mashed FRESH FRUIT
1 tsp. LEMON JUICE

Garlic

2 CLOVES GARLIC, mashed
1 1/2 Tbsp. minced PARSLEY

GARLIC

Herbs

1 Tbsp. chopped CHIVES
2 tsp. chopped CHERVIL
1 tsp. LEMON JUICE

BOUQUET GARNI

Mustard

2 Tbsp. DIJON-STYLE MUSTARD
1 Tbsp. LEMON JUICE
1 Tbsp. chopped GREEN ONIONS
   or CHIVES
PEPPER, a sprinkling

Onion

1/4 cup chopped fine RED ONION
1 Tbsp. RED WINE VINEGAR

Parsley, Rosemary & Thyme

1 Tbsp. LEMON JUICE
1 tsp. chopped PARSLEY
1/2 tsp. ROSEMARY
1/4 tsp. THYME

Tarragon

1 tsp. TARRAGON
1 Tbsp. SOUR CREAM
1 tsp. MAYONNAISE

Flavored Spreads

Combine and blend until smooth:

8 oz. CREAM CHEESE or WHIPPED CREAM CHEESE,
   at room temperature
1 tsp. VANILLA
1 cup grated WALNUTS
1 Tbsp. POWDERED SUGAR

(See also"Toppings" in index)

Muffins

A. M. Bacon Muffins

Sift together:
2 cups FLOUR
1 Tbsp. BAKING POWDER
2 Tbsp. SUGAR
1/2 tsp. SALT

Combine:
1 EGG, beaten
1 cup MILK
1/4 cup SALAD OIL

Combine mixtures until just moistened.

Add:
1/2 cup chopped, crisp BACON

Pour into sprayed muffin tins about 2/3 full. Makes approximately 16 muffins. Bake at 400° for 20 minutes.

Applesauce-Bran Muffins

Combine:
>   1 1/4 cups BRAN CEREAL
>   1 1/4 cups MILK

Add:
>   1 EGG
>   1/3 cup APPLESAUCE
>   1/2 cup minced APPLE
>   1/3 cup melted BUTTER or MARGARINE

Mix together:
>   1 1/4 cups flour
>   3 tsp. BAKING POWDER
>   1/2 tsp. SALT
>   1/2 cup BROWN SUGAR

Combine mixtures until just blended.
Add:
>   1/2 cup chopped PECANS

Fill sprayed muffin pans 2/3 full. Bake at 400° for 25 minutes.

Apricot-Bran Muffins

Combine and let stand 10 minutes:
>   2/3 cup finely chopped DRIED APRICOTS
>   Boiling WATER to cover

Drain and mix with:
>   2 Tbsp. SUGAR

Sift together:
>   1 cup FLOUR
>   1/3 cup SUGAR
>   2 1/2 tsp. BAKING POWDER
>   3/4 tsp. SALT

Mix together:
>   1 cup whole BRAN CEREAL
>   3/4 cup MILK
>   1 EGG, beaten
>   1/4 cup SALAD OIL

Combine flour and bran mixtures until just moistened. Stir in apricots. Fill sprayed muffin pans 2/3 full. Bake at 400° for 25 minutes. Makes a dozen muffins.

Banana Muffins

Mix together:
   2 cups FLOUR
   2 tsp. BAKING POWDER
   1/2 tsp. BAKING SODA
   1/2 tsp. SALT
   1/4 cup SUGAR

Combine:
   2 Tbsp. melted BUTTER
   1 mashed BANANA
   2 EGG YOLKS
   2/3 cup MILK
   1/4 cup chopped WALNUTS

Combine mixtures.

Fold in:
   2 EGG WHITES, stiffly beaten with:
   1/3 cup SUGAR

Pour into sprayed muffin pan. Makes a dozen muffins. Bake at 400° for 15 to 20 minutes.

Blueberry Muffins

Combine:
   1 EGG, beaten
   1/2 cup MILK
   1/2 cup BUTTER, room temperature
   1 tsp. grated LEMON PEEL

Mix together:
   1 1/2 cups FLOUR
   1/2 cup SUGAR
   2 tsp. BAKING POWDER
   1/2 tsp. SALT

Combine flour mixture with liquids until just moist.

Fold in:
   1 cup BLUEBERRIES, well drained.

Fill sprayed muffin tins about 3/4 full. Bake at 400° for 20 to 25 minutes.

Blueberry-Bran Muffins

Combine:
> **1/2 cup melted BUTTER**
> **1/2 cup MILK**
> **2 EGGS, beaten**

Sift together:
> **1 1/2 cups FLOUR**
> **1/2 cup SUGAR**
> **2 tsp. BAKING POWDER**
> **1/4 tsp. SALT**

Stir in:
> **1/2 cup BRAN or 3/4 cup BRAN FLAKES**
> **3/4 cup chopped NUTS, or toasted SUNFLOWER SEEDS**

Fold in:
> **1 1/2 cups rinsed and drained BLUEBERRIES**

Add dry ingredients to butter mixture until just moist. Spoon batter into sprayed muffin tin. Bake at 400° for 20 to 25 minutes.

Bran Muffins

Sift together:
> **1 1/2 cups FLOUR**
> **1 Tbsp. BAKING POWDER**
> **1/2 tsp. SALT**
> **1/4 cup SUGAR**

Combine and let stand a couple of minutes:
> **1 cup BRAN CEREAL**
> **1 cup MILK**

Add:
> **1 EGG**
> **3 Tbsp. SALAD OIL or melted BUTTER**

Combine mixtures until just moist. Add nuts or raisins, if desired. Spoon into sprayed muffin pans. Bake at 400° for 20 to 25 minutes.

Bran-Apple Muffins

Combine and soak:
1 1/2 cups BRAN BUD CEREAL
1 1/4 cups MILK

Mix together:
1 1/4 cups FLOUR
1 Tbsp. BAKING POWDER
1/2 tsp. SALT
1/2 cup BROWN SUGAR

Combine:
1 EGG, lightly beaten
1/3 cup MARGARINE or BUTTER, melted
1/3 cup APPLESAUCE
1/2 cup chopped tart APPLE

Add cereal mixture and dry ingredients. Mix until just moist. Spoon into sprayed muffin pan. Bake at 400° for 25 minutes.

Bran-Raisin Muffins

Melt:
1/3 cup BUTTER

Add, in order:
1/2 cup firmly packed BROWN SUGAR
1/4 cup MOLASSES
2 EGGS
1 cup MILK

Mix together:
1 1/2 cups BRAN
1 cup FLOUR
1 1/2 tsp. BAKING SODA
3/4 tsp. SALT

Combine mixtures and fold in:
1/2 cup RAISINS

Spoon into paper-lined or sprayed muffin tins. Bake at 400° for 15 to 20 minutes.

Bran-Wheat Muffins

Mix together:
1 1/2 cups FLOUR
1 cup BRAN CEREAL
1 tsp. SALT
1 1/2 tsp. BAKING SODA
3/4 cup SUGAR

Combine and let stand 10 to 20 minutes:
3/4 cup SHREDDED WHEAT
1 cup boiling WATER

Cream:
1/2 cup BUTTER, room temperature
2 EGGS

Add:
1 cup BUTTERMILK or YOGURT

Combine all mixtures until just blended. Spoon into sprayed or paper-lined muffin pans. Bake at 400° for 20 to 25 minutes.

Buttermilk-Bran Muffins

Combine:
1 cup WHEAT FLOUR
1 cup FLOUR
1/3 cup BRAN FLAKES
1 tsp. BAKING SODA
1 tsp. SALT

Combine:
1 cup BUTTERMILK
1 Tbsp. SALAD OIL
1/3 cup HONEY

Combine mixtures until just blended, then add:
1/2 cup finely chopped NUTS

Pour into 2 sprayed 8 x 4 loaf pans. Bake at 350° for one hour. If you double this recipe it will make about 18 muffins. Then bake at 375° for 20 minutes.

Carrot-Bran Muffins

Combine:
1/2 cup FLOUR
1 1/2 cups BRAN
1 cup WHEAT FLOUR
1/4 cup WHEAT GERM
1 tsp. BAKING POWDER
3/4 tsp. BAKING SODA
1/2 tsp. SALT

Combine:
1 EGG, beaten
3/4 cup MILK
1/2 cup HONEY
4 Tbsp. melted BUTTER or MARGARINE

Combine mixtures until just blended and stir in:
1 cup shredded or puréed CARROTS
1/2 cup chopped NUTS

Fill sprayed muffin pans 3/4 full. Bake at 400° for 20 minutes. Makes 18 muffins.

Cinnamon Muffins

Cream:
1/2 cup BUTTER or MARGARINE, room temperature
1/2 cup SUGAR

Add:
1 EGG
1/2 cup MILK

Mix together:
1 1/2 cups FLOUR
1 1/2 tsp. BAKING POWDER
1 1/2 tsp. CINNAMON
1/2 tsp. SALT
1/4 tsp. NUTMEG

Combine the mixtures until just moist and fold in:
3/4 cup chopped NUTS

Spoon into sprayed muffin tins. Bake at 350° for 20 to 25 minutes.

Coffee Muffins

Mix together:
> **1 cup sifted FLOUR**
> **1 tsp. BAKING POWDER**
> **1/2 tsp. SALT**

Separate and beat yolks until light, gradually adding sugar:
> **3 EGGS**
> **1/4 cup SUGAR**

Fold into flour mixture and add:
> **1/2 cup COFFEE**

Beat the egg whites until light and gradually add:
> **1/3 cup SUGAR**

Fold into flour / egg yolk mixture and add:
> **1/2 cup sliced, toasted ALMONDS**

Spoon into sprayed muffin tins. Bake at 375° for 25 minutes.

Cornmeal-Blueberry Muffins

Combine:
> **1 cup FLOUR**
> **2/3 cup CORNMEAL**
> **1/3 cup SUGAR**
> **2 tsp. BAKING POWDER**
> **1/2 tsp. BAKING SODA**
> **1/2 tsp. SALT**

Mix together:
> **3 EGGS, beaten**
> **1 cup BUTTERMILK or YOGURT**
> **1/4 cup BUTTER, melted**

Combine mixtures until just moist.

Fold in:
> **1 1/3 cups rinsed and drained BLUEBERRIES**

Spoon into sprayed muffin pans. Bake at 400° for 20 minutes. Makes about one dozen muffins.

Date Muffins

Sift together:
> 1 1/2 cups FLOUR
> 2 tsp. BAKING POWDER
> 1/2 tsp. SALT

Cream together:
> 6 Tbsp. BUTTER or MARGARINE, softened
> 2/3 cup BROWN SUGAR

Add and mix well:
> 1 EGG
> 1/2 cup MILK
> 1 tsp. VANILLA

Combine mixtures until just moistened then stir in:
> 1 cup chopped fine DATES
> 1 cup chopped RAISINS

Pour into sprayed muffin pans. Makes approximately 12 muffins. Bake at 400° for 20 to 25 minutes.

Date-Applesauce Muffins

Cream:
> 1/2 cup BUTTER or MARGARINE, room temperature

Gradually add:
> 3/4 cup HONEY
> 1 EGG
> 1 tsp. VANILLA
> 1 cup APPLESAUCE

Combine:
> 1 cup FLOUR
> 1 cup WHOLE WHEAT FLOUR
> 1 tsp. BAKING SODA
> 1/2 tsp. SALT
> 1/2 tsp. CINNAMON
> 1/4 tsp. GROUND CLOVES
> 1/4 tsp. NUTMEG
> 1/8 tsp. GINGER

Combine mixtures until blended and stir in:
> 1 cup chopped DATES
> 3/4 cup chopped WALNUTS or PECANS

Spoon into sprayed muffin pans about 3/4 full. Makes about 24 muffins. Bake at 350° for 30 minutes.

Date-Bran Muffins

Combine:
    1 cup BRAN CEREAL KERNELS
    1 cup BUTTERMILK or YOGURT

Mix together:
    1 cup FLOUR
    1 tsp. CINNAMON
    1 tsp. BAKING POWDER
    1/2 tsp. SALT
    1/2 tsp. BAKING SODA

Cream:
    1/3 cup BUTTER, room temperature
    1/2 cup BROWN SUGAR

Add and mix thoroughly:
    1 EGG
    1/4 cup MOLASSES

Combine the three mixtures then stir in:
    1/3 cup RAISINS
    1/3 cup chopped fine DATES
    1/3 cup chopped WALNUTS

Fill sprayed muffin pans 3/4 full. Makes approximately 12 muffins. Bake at 400° for 20 to 25 minutes.

Fruit Cocktail Muffins

Mix together:
    2 cups FLOUR
    2 tsp. BAKING POWDER
    1/2 tsp. BAKING SODA
    1/2 tsp. SALT
    1/3 cup SUGAR
    1/2 tsp. CINNAMON

Combine:
    1 EGG, beaten
    2/3 cup MILK
    1/2 tsp. grated ORANGE PEEL

Combine two mixtures until just moistened and stir in:
    1 cup drained and chopped FRUIT COCKTAIL

Spoon into sprayed muffin pans. Bake at 400° for 20 minutes.

Fruit with Bran Muffins

Combine:
> 1 1/4 cups BRAN KERNELS
> 1/2 cup boiling WATER

Cool until lukewarm.

Add:
> 1 EGG, beaten
> 1 cup BUTTERMILK or YOGURT
> 1/2 cup HONEY
> 1/4 cup BUTTER, melted

Mix together:
> 1 cup FLOUR
> 1/2 cup WHOLE WHEAT FLOUR
> 1 tsp. BAKING POWDER
> 1 tsp. BAKING SODA
> 1/2 tsp. SALT

Combine mixtures until just moistened and stir in:
> 1 1/2 cups chopped DRIED PRUNES and/or APRICOTS
> 1/2 cup chopped NUTS

Spoon into sprayed muffin pans about 3/4 full. Bake at 425° for 20 minutes.

Granola Muffins

Mix together:
> 1 1/2 cups FLOUR
> 1/2 cup WHEAT FLOUR
> 1 cup GRANOLA
>   WITH RAISINS
> 1/2 cup BROWN SUGAR
> 1 Tbsp. BAKING POWDER
> 1/4 tsp. SALT

Combine:
> 1 EGG, beaten
> 1 cup MILK
> 1/2 cup SALAD OIL or BUTTER, melted

Combine mixtures until just moistened. Stir in:
> 1/2 cup chopped WALNUTS

Spoon into sprayed muffin pans. Makes 12 muffins. Bake at 400° for 20 to 25 minutes.

Ice Cream Muffins

Combine:

2 cups self-rising FLOUR
2 cups VANILLA ICE CREAM, softened
1 EGG, beaten
1/4 cup SALAD OIL

Spoon into sprayed muffin pans, 2/3 full. Bake at 400° for 20 minutes. This easy-to-prepare recipe is ideal for the mini-muffin pans. There's a nice, light taste of vanilla ice cream

Lemonade Muffins

Sift together:
2 cups FLOUR
1/4 cup SUGAR
2 1/2 tsp. BAKING POWDER
1/2 tsp. SALT

Combine:
1 EGG, beaten
1/2 cup FROZEN LEMONADE CONCENTRATE, thawed
1/4 cup WATER
1/3 cup SALAD OIL

Combine mixtures until just moistened and stir in:
1/2 cup chopped WALNUTS

Fill sprayed muffin pans 2/3 full. Bake at 400° for 25 minutes. Makes 12 muffins.

Lemonade Topping

Combine:
2 Tbsp. LEMONADE CONCENTRATE
1 Tbsp. SUGAR

Brush on tops of muffins while hot.

Mandarin Orange Muffins

Mix together:
>   2 cups FLOUR
>   1 tsp. CINNAMON
>   1/2 tsp. SALT
>   1 tsp. BAKING POWDER
>   1/2 tsp. GROUND CARDAMOM
>   3/4 tsp. MACE

Combine:
>   2 EGGS, beaten
>   1 cup SUGAR
>   3/4 cup SALAD OIL
>   1/2 cup CREAM
>   1 cup MANDARIN ORANGES, drained and dry

Combine mixtures until just moist. Spoon into sprayed muffin pans about 2/3 full. Bake at 350° for 30 minutes. Makes a generous 12 muffins.

Nutmeg Muffins

Mix together:
>   2 cups FLOUR
>   3/4 cup SUGAR
>   1 Tbsp. BAKING POWDER
>   1 1/2 Tbsp. freshly grated NUTMEG
>   1/2 tsp. SALT

Combine:
>   2 EGGS, beaten
>   1 1/2 cups HALF AND HALF
>   1/2 cup BUTTER, melted

Combine mixtures until just moistened. Spoon into sprayed muffin tin. Bake at 400° for 20 minutes. Makes 12 muffins.

Oat-Apple Muffins

Mix together:
1 cup ROLLED OATS, toasted
1/2 cup BRAN or OAT CEREAL with DRIED FRUITS

Mix together:
1 cup FLOUR
2 Tbsp. BAKING POWDER
1 tsp. CINNAMON

Mix together:
2 EGGS, beaten
1/4 cup SALAD OIL
1/2 cup BROWN SUGAR
3/4 cup MILK
1 cup chopped APPLES or 3/4 cup APPLESAUCE

Combine all mixtures until just moistened. Spoon in sprayed muffin pans. Bake at 400° for 20 minutes.

Oat-Buttermilk Muffins

Mix together:
1 cup WHEAT FLOUR
1 cup ROLLED OATS
1 tsp. BAKING SODA
1/2 tsp. SALT

Combine:
2 EGGS, beaten
1 cup BUTTERMILK
1/4 cup SALAD OIL
3/4 cup BROWN SUGAR

Combine mixtures until just moistened and stir in:
1 cup RAISINS

Spoon into sprayed muffin pans. Bake at 400° for 15 to 20 minutes.

Oat-Cranberry Muffins

Mix together:
1 cup WHEAT FLOUR
1/2 cup FLOUR
1 cup QUICK OATS

1 Tbsp. BAKING POWDER
1 tsp. SALT
1/2 tsp. CINNAMON

Mix together:
1 EGG, beaten
4 Tbsp. BUTTER, melted
1 cup MILK

1/2 cup BROWN SUGAR
1 cup CRANBERRY SAUCE

Combine mixtures until just moistened.

Stir in:
1 cup chopped NUTS

Spoon into sprayed muffin pans. Bake at 375° for 20 minutes.

Prune-Carrot Muffins

Cream:
1/2 cup BUTTER or MARGARINE, room temperature

Beat in:
1/2 cup BROWN SUGAR

Add:
2 EGGS, one at a time
3/4 tsp. VANILLA
3/4 cup shredded CARROTS
1/3 cup ORANGE JUICE

Mix together:
1 1/2 cup FLOUR
3/4 tsp. BAKING SODA
3/4 tsp. CINNAMON

1/2 tsp. SALT
1/4 tsp. NUTMEG
1/8 tsp. GROUND CLOVES

Combine mixtures until just moistened and stir in:
1/2 cup chopped WALNUTS
1/2 cup chopped PRUNES

Fill sprayed muffin pans 3/4 full. Bake at 350° for 3 minutes.
Makes 18 muffins.

Sour Cream Muffins

Mix together:
2 cups FLOUR
1 Tbsp. BAKING POWDER
1 tsp. BAKING SODA
1/2 tsp. SALT
1 tsp. CINNAMON
1/3 cup SUGAR
1/3 cup BROWN SUGAR
1 1/2 tsp. grated ORANGE PEEL

Combine:
1 cup SOUR CREAM
1/3 cup ORANGE JUICE
1 EGG, beaten
1/2 cup BUTTER, melted

Combine mixtures until just moistened.
Stir in:
1/2 cup chopped NUTS
Spoon into sprayed muffin pans 2/3 full. Bake at 400° for 20 minutes.

Sour Cream-Date Muffins

Sift together:
2 cups FLOUR
1/2 cup BROWN SUGAR
2 tsp. BAKING POWDER
1/2 tsp. BAKING SODA
1/2 tsp. SALT

Combine:
1 EGG, beaten
1 cup SOUR CREAM
1/2 cup MILK
4 Tbsp. BUTTER or MARGARINE, melted
1 Tbsp. INSTANT COFFEE POWDER

Combine mixtures until just moist then stir in:
1 cup finely chopped DATES

Fill sprayed muffin pans 2/3 full. Makes about 12 muffins.
Bake at 400° for 20 to 25 minutes.

Variety Breads

Basic Biscuits

Sift together:
2 cups FLOUR, white or wheat
1 Tbsp. BAKING POWDER
1/2 tsp. SUGAR
1/2 tsp. SALT

Cut in until as fine as coarse salt:
1/4 cup SHORTENING or LARD

Add enough milk to make soft dough:
2/3 to 3/4 cup MILK

Roll 1/2" thick on lightly floured board. Cut with floured cutter.
Place close together for soft sides on ungreased baking sheet.
Bake at 450° for 10 to 12 minutes until golden brown.

Biscuit Variations

Buttermilk Biscuits

BUTTERMILK — substitute for milk
Add:
    1/4 tsp. BAKING SODA
    Reduce to 2 tsp. BAKING POWDER
Bake 450° for 10 to 12 minutes

Cinnamon Rolls

Dip biscuits into:
    1/4 cup melted BUTTER
Roll in mixture of:
    1/4 cup SUGAR mixed with 2 Tbsp. CINNAMON
Place in cake or pie pan. Pour rest of butter over top. Bake at 400° for 15 minutes.

Pancakes

Increase MILK or thin with a little WATER
Add:
    1 to 2 EGGS, beaten
Just blend; drop by spoonfuls on hot griddle

Tuna Roll

Roll biscuit dough into 1/4" thick rectangle. Spread with mixture of:

1 can TUNA, drained and flaked	**1 tsp. minced PIMENTO**
	2 Tbsp. MAYONNAISE
1 Tbsp. CHIVES	**1 Tbsp. LEMON JUICE**
1 tsp. minced ONION	

Roll up dough, like a jelly roll, pinch edges together to seal and cut into 1-1/4" slices. Place on sprayed baking sheet. Bake at 400° for 15 to 20 minutes.

Whipped Cream Biscuits

Sift together:
    1 1/2 cups FLOUR
    4 tsp. BAKING POWDER
    1/2 tsp. SALT

Blend into flour mixture:
    1 cup HEAVY CREAM, whipped

Roll out and bake as directed in biscuit recipe on previous page.

Corn Bread

Mix together:
- **1/2 cup FLOUR**
- **1/2 cup CORNMEAL**
- **2 Tbsp. SUGAR**
- **1 1/2 tsp. BAKING POWDER**
- **1/2 tsp. SALT**

Cut in:
- **3 Tbsp. MARGARINE**

Beat and add:
- **1 EGG**
- **1/2 cup MILK**

Mix until just blended. Pour into sprayed 8" square baking dish. Bake at 400° for 15 to 20 minutes.

Serve These Hot!

Corn-Buttermilk Bread

Cream:
- **1/2 cup BUTTER, room temperature**
- **1/2 cup SUGAR**

Add:
- **2 EGGS, beaten**
- **1 cup BUTTERMILK**

Combine:
- **1 cup CORNMEAL**
- **1 cup FLOUR**
- **1/2 tsp. SALT**

Combine mixtures until just moistened. Pour into sprayed 8" square baking dish. Bake at 375° for 35 minutes.

Corn Custard

Combine:
> **1/2 cup FLOUR**
> **3/4 cup YELLOW CORNMEAL**
> **1 tsp. BAKING POWDER**
> **1/2 tsp. SALT**
> **2 1/2 Tbsp. BROWN SUGAR**

Combine:
> **1 EGG, beaten**
> **2 Tbsp. BUTTER, melted**
> **1 cup MILK**

Combine mixtures and pour batter into sprayed 8" square baking dish.

Spoon on top of batter to float:
> **1/2 cup MILK**

Bake at 400° for 20 minutes. Serve hot!

Corn Sticks

Mix together:
> **1 cup FLOUR**
> **1 cup YELLOW CORNMEAL**
> **1 Tbsp. BAKING POWDER**
> **3/4 tsp. SALT**

Combine:
> **2 EGGS, beaten**
> **1/2 cup PARMESAN CHEESE (optional)**
> **1/3 cup SALAD OIL**
> **1 cup MILK**
> **1/3 cup CREAMED CORN (optional)**

Combine mixtures until just moist. Spoon into sprayed corn stick pan using 2 to 3 tablespoons of batter per stick. Bake at 400° for 20 minutes.

Corn-Maple Syrup Bread

Mix together:
- 1 cup YELLOW CORNMEAL
- 1 cup FLOUR
- 1 tsp. BAKING POWDER
- 1 tsp. BAKING SODA
- 1 tsp. SALT
- 2 Tbsp. BROWN SUGAR

Mix together:
- 3 EGGS, beaten
- 1/3 cup MAPLE SYRUP
- 1/2 cup MILK

Combine Mixtures.

Fold in:
- 1/2 cup chopped NUTS

Pour into sprayed 8" square baking dish. Bake at 400° for 20 minutes. Serve hot!

Mexican Corn Bread

Mix together:
- 1 cup YELLOW CORNMEAL
- 1 cup FLOUR
- 1 Tbsp. BAKING POWDER
- 1/2 tsp. PAPRIKA
- 1/2 tsp. SALT

Mix together:
- 2 EGGS, beaten
- 1/4 cup SALAD OIL
- 1 cup MILK
- 1 cup CORN (creamed or kernels)
- 1/2 cup chopped GREEN CHILES
- 2 Tbsp. chopped PIMENTO
- 1/2 cup shredded or grated Jack or Cheddar CHEESE

Combine mixtures until just moistened. Pour into sprayed 8" square baking dish. Bake at 400° for 30 minutes.

Nut Roll

Beat:
4 EGG YOLKS

Add:
1/4 cup SUGAR

Beat:
4 EGG WHITES, to soft peaks

Fold yolk mixture into whites.

Sift together and fold in:
1/3 cup FLOUR
1 tsp. BAKING POWDER

Fold in:
3/4 cup ground WALNUTS or CASHEWS
or ALMONDS or PECAN
1 Tbsp. grated LEMON PEEL

Spread into sprayed 14 x 10 x 1 jelly roll pan. Bake at 375° for 12 minutes. Turn out on towel dusted with confectioners sugar. Roll up in towel. Allow to cool. Unroll, spread with filling. Reroll.

Fillings

- **Butter creams, flavored**
- **Cheese or meat spreads**
- **Creamed cheese, whipped with a flavoring**
- **Jams or preserves**
- **Whipped cream with fruit**
- **Whipped cream with ice cream and nuts**
- **Decorate roll with additional filling and nuts**

Oatcakes

Combine:
>**1/3 cup FLOUR**
>**1 tsp. BAKING POWDER**
>**1/4 tsp. SALT**
>**1/2 tsp. SUGAR**

Add:
>**1 1/2 cups ground QUICK ROLLED OATS***

*Grind to a coarse consistency in food processor.

Work in:
>**2 1/2 Tbsp. MARGARINE or LARD (cold)**

Add:
>**1/3 cup MILK or cold WATER**

Form into a ball. Roll on floured surface to 1/4" thickness. Cut with 2 1/2" cookie or biscuit cutter. Place on sprayed baking sheet. Bake at 375° for 20 minutes. Makes 15 oatcakes.

Parmesan Wafers

Blend well:
>**1 1/2 cups grated PARMESAN CHEESE**
>**1 cup FLOUR**
>**1/2 cup BUTTER, room temperature**
>**3/4 tsp. OREGANO**
>**1/2 tsp. MARJORAM**
>**1/2 tsp. BASIL**

Add:
>**1/2 tsp. WORCESTERSHIRE SAUCE**
>**3 Tbsp. DRY WHITE WINE**

Form into two logs approximately 1 1/2" in diameter. Wrap and refrigerate. Cut 1/4" slices and place 1/2" apart on sprayed baking sheet. Bake at 400° for 12 to 15 minutes. Serve hot. Makes about 4 dozen wafers.

Popovers

Combine in mixer in order shown and beat until smooth:
3 EGGS
1 cup MILK
1 Tbsp. SALAD OIL
1/4 tsp. SALT
1 cup FLOUR

Fill every other cup of sprayed muffin pan. Makes 6. Bake at 375° a little more than one hour. Pierce each popover in several places five minutes before removing from oven.

Sausage Loaves

Mix together:
2 cups FLOUR
3 Tbsp. grated PARMESAN CHEESE
2 Tbsp. BROWN SUGAR
1 Tbsp. SUGAR
1 Tbsp. BAKING POWDER
1/2 tsp. BAKING SODA
1/2 tsp. SALT
1 tsp. CARAWAY SEED

Combine:
1 cup WHIPPED CREAM CHEESE
3/4 cup MILK
2 EGGS, one at a time
2 Tbsp. BUTTER, melted
1 cup crumbled or chopped SAUSAGE*

*Dry chorizo or pepperoni or fresh sausage, crumbled and stir-fried until crisp and then drained.

Combine mixtures until just moistened and spoon into 3 sprayed 8 x 4 loaf pans. Bake at 375° for 45 to 50 minutes.

Scones

Mix together:
> **3 cups FLOUR**
> **2 tsp. BAKING SODA**
> **1/2 tsp. SALT**
> **1/2 cup SUGAR**
> **1 tsp. grated ORANGE PEEL**

Cut in:
> **1/2 cup cold BUTTER or MARGARINE**

Work in:
> **1 EGG, beaten**
> **1/2 cup CREAM or EVAPORATED MILK**

Knead and form into a ball. Pat down and roll to 1/3" to 1/2" thickness. Cut into rounds, wedges or squares. Place on sprayed baking sheet. Bake at 400° for 15 to 20 minutes. Sprinkle with **POWDERED SUGAR.**

Scones with Buttermilk

Mix together:
> **3 cups FLOUR**
> **1 Tbsp. BAKING POWDER**
> **1/2 tsp. BAKING SODA**
> **1/2 tsp. SALT**
> **1/2 cup SUGAR**
> **1/4 tsp. CINNAMON**
> **1/4 tsp. NUTMEG**

Cut in:
> **1/2 cup cold BUTTER**

Work in:
> **1 cup BUTTERMILK**
> **1/2 cup chopped NUTS or RAISINS**

Knead and form into a ball. Pat down, roll or shape to 1/2" thickness. Cut into 3" to 4" rounds. Place on sprayed baking sheet. Bake at 400° for 20 minutes. Sprinkle with **POWDERED SUGAR.**

Scones with Herbs

Mix together:
>   3 cups FLOUR
>   1/4 cup SUGAR
>   2 tsp. BAKING POWDER
>   1 tsp. CELERY SEED
>   1/2 tsp. DILL SEED
>   1/2 tsp. THYME
>   1/2 tsp. ROSEMARY

Cut in:
>   1/2 cup cold BUTTER or MARGARINE

Work in:
>   1 EGG, beaten
>   1/2 cup BUTTERMILK or YOGURT

Knead and form into a ball. Pat down into 1/2" thickness. Form into circle and cut wedges or cut into rounds. Place on sprayed baking sheet. Bake at 400° for 20 minutes.

Orange Scones

Sift together:
>   2 1/2 cups FLOUR
>   1 tsp. BAKING SODA
>   1 Tbsp. BAKING POWDER
>   1/2 tsp. SALT
>   2 Tbsp. SUGAR

Cut in:
>   1/2 cup BUTTER or MARGARINE

Combine:
>   3/4 cups ORANGE JUICE
>   3 Tbsp. LEMON JUICE
>   1 EGG, beaten

Combine mixtures. Form into ball. Roll to 1/4" and cut with 2 1/2" cookie or biscuit cutter. Place on sprayed baking sheet, brush tops with milk and sprinkle with sugar. Bake at 425° for 10 to 13 minutes.

Scones with Raisins

Mix together:
2 cups WHEAT FLOUR
1 Tbsp. BAKING POWDER
1/3 cup SUGAR
1 tsp. grated ORANGE PEEL

Cut in:
1/2 cup cold BUTTER or MARGARINE

Work in:
3/4 cup RAISINS
1/2 cup MILK or HALF AND HALF

Knead and form into a ball. Pat down and roll to 1/2" thickness. Cut into rounds. Crimp edges, if desired. Place on sprayed baking sheet. Bake at 400° for 20 minutes. Sprinkle with **POWDERED SUGAR.**

Spiced Scones

Mix together:
3 cups FLOUR
1 Tbsp. BAKING POWDER
1/2 tsp. BAKING SODA
1/2 tsp. SALT
1/2 cup SUGAR
2 tsp. CINNAMON
1/2 tsp. NUTMEG
1/2 tsp. ALLSPICE

Only 15 - 20 minutes in the oven!

Cut in:
3/4 cup cold BUTTER

Work in:
3/4 cup BUTTERMILK or LIGHT CREAM or YOGURT
1/2 cup chopped NUTS

Knead and form into a ball. Pat down and roll into 1/2" or less thickness. Cut into rounds. Crimp edges. Place on sprayed baking sheet. Bake at 400° for 15 to 20 minutes. Sprinkle with **POWDERED SUGAR.**

Shortbread

Mix together:
  2 cups FLOUR
  1/4 tsp. SALT
  1/2 tsp. BAKING POWDER

Cream until fluffy:
  1 cup BUTTER, room temperature
  1/2 cup POWDERED SUGAR

Add flour mixture.

Roll to 1/3" thickness. Cut into rounds or squares. Crimp edges. Prick deeply with fork. Place on sprayed baking sheet. Bake at 350° for 5 minutes, then reduce and bake at 300° for 20 minutes.

Spoon Bread

Mix together:
  1 cup YELLOW CORNMEAL
  1/2 cup FLOUR
  1 tsp. SALT
  1 Tbsp. BAKING POWDER

Mix together:
  4 EGG YOLKS, beaten
  2 Tbsp. BUTTER or MARGARINE, melted
  1 cup MILK
  1/2 cup BACON BITS (or crisp bacon crumbled)
  1 1/2 cups grated or shredded CHEDDAR CHEESE
  1/2 cup chopped PIMENTOS

Combine mixtures until just moist.

Fold in:
  4 EGG WHITES, beaten until forms peak

Spoon into sprayed 9" square baking dish. Bake at 400° for 30 minutes.

Sunflower Mini-Loaves

Mix together:
2 cups FLOUR
3/4 cup WHEAT FLOUR
2 Tbsp. SUGAR
1 tsp. BAKING SODA
1/2 tsp. SALT

Combine:
1 EGG, beaten
1 1/2 cups YOGURT or BUTTERMILK
1/4 cup BUTTER, melted

Combine mixtures until just moistened.

Stir in:
1/2 cup shelled, roasted SUNFLOWER SEEDS

Knead lightly, pat down and roll to 1/2" thickness. Cut in rounds or squares. Place on sprayed baking sheet. Bake at 400° for 15 to 20 minutes.

Swiss Cheese Bread

Heat until butter is melted:
1/3 cup BUTTER
1 cup MILK

Beat in:
1/4 tsp. SALT
1 cup FLOUR

Beat in one at a time; beating constantly. Remove pan from heat after each addition:
4 EGGS

Remove from heat and blend in:
1/2 cup grated or shredded SWISS CHEESE
1/8 tsp. DRY MUSTARD
1/2 tsp. minced ONION

Mound on 10" sprayed pie plate. Sprinkle on top:
3 Tbsp. grated SWISS CHEESE

Bake at 375° for 20 minutes, then reduce to 350° and bake for 20 minutes. Serve hot.

General Information

Baking powder and baking soda: These are the ingredients that make these breads faster to prepare than yeast breads. Buy the smallest can of baking powder available as it gradually loses its strength. Do not keep after five months. Baking powder begins to act as soon as liquid is added, so the breads should go into the preheated oven as soon as batter is mixed and spooned into pans or tins.

Baking times: Adjust baking time to size of pan. One large standard loaf will divide into two disposable foil pans, cutting 10 to 15 minutes from baking time. Most recipes will adapt to muffins or pan sizes other than those stated in recipes.

Substitutions:
- 1 cup Buttermilk—mix 6 tbsp. powdered buttermilk and 1 cup water.
- Sour milk—add 1 tbsp. vinegar to 1 cup milk (at room temperature). Allow to sit 5 minutes
- Brown sugar for white
- Sunflower seeds for nuts
- 3/4 cup whole wheat flour and 1/4 cup wheat germ for 1 cup flour
- Yogurt for buttermilk.

Can sizes:
303 =	2 cups	(16-17 oz.)
300 =	1 3/4 cups	(14-16 oz.)
2 =	2 1/2 cups	(1 lb. 4 oz.—1 pint 2 fl. oz.)
2 1/2 =	3 1/2 cups	(1 lb. 13 oz.)

Cooling: Cool loaves 10 minutes in pans after removing from oven. Place on rack and allow to cool thoroughly for one hour. Wrap or seal in plastic bag as free of air as possible.

Grating: When grating oranges, lemons or limes, use just the colored part of the peel as the white under layer gives a bitter flavor.

High altitudes:
- Reduce baking powder and soda 1/8 to 1/4 teaspoon per teaspoon
- Reduce sugar 1 to 2 tablespoons per cup
- Increase liquids 2 to 4 tablespoons per cup
- Increase oven temperature 15° to 25°

Ovens, Convection and Microwave: Recipes are given for use in standard ovens, however for shorter baking times use microwave or convection ovens.

When adapting to microwave, round dishes or casseroles will be more satisfactory containers for even baking of breads or muffins. The use of a turntable will also add to the baking efficiency of the microwave. Fill muffin papers, custard cups or dishes little more than half full as batter rises higher than in a conventional oven. Breads do not brown, so use the more colorful breads for microwave cooking.

Microwave one cupcake: 30 to 40 seconds

Microwave loaves: **50 percent power** about 6 minutes *(rotating by round table or every 3 minutes by hand) then at* **High power** *about 3 minutes*

Convection baking of nut breads and muffins uses a reduced temperature from the conventional radiant ovens. Generally reduce the temperature by 25°. Also place loaf pans and muffin pans lengthwise in oven, front to back, for better air circulation and browning. Baking time will be pretty close to the same time specified. Use the toothpick test for doneness.

Pan preparation: Spray pans with vegetable cooking spray rather than grease or butter or lining pans. Breads will slip out of pan easily after 10 minutes cooling.

Pan sizes: Recipes with at least 2 cups of flour will fit in 9 x 5 pan or will divide into smaller pans. The smaller disposable pan sizes are approximately 8 x 4 and 6 x 3.

Preparation: Most quick breads should be mixed with a light folding motion until the flour mixture is just moistened. Many of these bread batters are quite thick and relatively dry so that the breads or muffins will be nicely rounded and the heavier ingredients will hold their place during baking. If nut breads are mixed too well, the top may be tough and pale and the inside may be full of holes. Overmixing can cause the bread to be tough and heavy as well.

Two speedy preparation tips:

- Get out all ingredients before mixing. Many ingredients can be measured before the mixing procedures begin.
- The dry and wet ingredients can be prepared the day before, then combined just before baking.

Store: Nut breads freeze beautifully for hostess gifts, holiday giving, potluck dinners or for meals at home. The breads can be stored in sealed plastic in the refrigerator for about a week.

Testing: Use toothpick test for doneness. It should come out clean.

Index

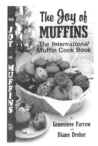

SALSA LOVERS COOK BOOK

More than 180 taste-tempting recipes for salsas that will make every meal a special event! Salsas for salads, appetizers, main dishes and desserts! Put some salsa in your life! By Susan K. Bollin.

5 1/2 x 8 1/2 — 128 pages . . . $5.95

CHIP & DIP LOVERS
COOK BOOK

More than 150 recipes for fun and festive dips. Make southwestern dips, dips with fruits and vegetables, meats, poultry and seafood. Salsa dips and dips for desserts. Includes recipes for making homemade chips. By Susan K. Bollin.

5 1/2 x 8 1/2 — 112 pages . . . $5.95

QUICK-N-EASY
MEXICAN RECIPES

More than 175 favorite Mexican recipes you can prepare in less than thirty minutes. Traditional items such as tacos, tostadas and enchiladas. Also features easy recipes for salads, soups, breads, desserts and drinks. By Susan K. Bollin.

5 1/2 x 8 1/2 — 128 pages . . . $5.95

PUMPKIN LOVERS
COOK BOOK

It's pumpkin time again! More than 175 recipes for soups, breads, muffins, pies, cakes, cheesecakes, cookies, ice cream, and more! Includes pumpkin trivia!

5 1/2 x 8 1/2—128 pages . . . $6.95

VEGGIE LOVERS COOK BOOK

Vegans will love these no cholesterol, no animal fat recipes! Over 200 nutritious, flavorful recipes by Chef Morty Star. Includes a foreword by Dr. Michael Klaper. Nutritional analyses for each recipe to help you plan a healthy diet.

5 1/2 x 8 1/2 — 128 pages . . . $6.95

ORDER BLANK

GOLDEN WEST PUBLISHERS

☼ 4113 N. Longview Ave. • Phoenix, AZ 85014

602-265-4392 • **1-800-658-5830** • FAX 602-279-6901

Qty	Title	Price	Amount
	Apple Lovers Cook Book	6.95	
	Best Barbecue Recipes	5.95	
	Chili-Lovers Cook Book	5.95	
	Chip and Dip Lovers Cook Book	5.95	
	Citrus Lovers Cook Book	6.95	
	Date Recipes	6.95	
	Easy RV Recipes	6.95	
	Easy Recipes for Wild Game & Fish	6.95	
	Joy of Muffins	5.95	
	Mexican Desserts & Drinks	6.95	
	Mexican Family Favorites Cook Book	5.95	
	Pecan-Lovers Cook Book	6.95	
	Pumpkin Recipes	6.95	
	Quick-Bread Cook Book	6.95	
	Quick-n-Easy Mexican Recipes	5.95	
	Recipes for a Healthy Lifestyle	6.95	
	Salsa Lovers Cook Book	5.95	
	Tequila Cook Book	7.95	
	Tortilla Lovers Cook Book	6.95	
	Veggie Lovers Cook Book	6.95	
Shipping & Handling Add ⟹	U.S. & Canada Other countries	$3.00 $5.00	

☐ My Check or Money Order Enclosed $

☐ MasterCard ☐ VISA ($20 credit card minimum)

(Payable in U.S. funds)

Acct. No.   Exp. Date

Signature

Name   Telephone

Address

City/State/Zip

Call for FREE catalog

1/97   Quick-Bread

This order blank may be photo-copied.